D0722410

Moses

Moses

A Memoir

Joel Cohen

Paulist Press
New York/Mahwah, N.J.

Jacket design by Cynthia Dunne
Jacket art: Guido Reni (1575–1642). *Moses with the Tablets of the Law.* Scala/Art Resource, NY.
Book design by Lynn Else

ISBN 0-8091-0558-6

Published by Paulist Press
997 Macarthur Boulevard
Mahwah, New Jersey 07430

www.paulistpress.com

Printed and bound in the United States of America

To the memory of
Nathan and Miriam Cohen,
who well embraced life's mosaic
and
To Eileen, the dark-skinned
beauty who, like Zipporah,
always inspires

"Every artist paints himself."
Cosimo de Medici

Contents

Foreword ix

Preface xv

Abbreviations xvii

Chapter 1: At Nebo 1

Chapter 2: Youth 6

Chapter 3: The Fugitive 12

Chapter 4: The Burning Bush 16

Chapter 5: The Return 21

Chapter 6: The Ten Plagues 27

Chapter 7: The Sea of Reeds 32

Chapter 8: The Decalogue 38

Chapter 9: Atop Sinai 53

Chapter 10: The Golden Calf 65

Chapter 11: Slaughter at Sinai 75

Chapter 12: The Mask 79

Chapter 13: Miriam 82

Chapter 14: The Spies 89

Chapter 15: Korah 95

Chapter 16: The Rock 106

Chapter 17: Interludes 113

Chapter 18: Dusk 123

Reflections on Moses after His Death 135

Glossary 148

*"Now the man Moses was very humble,
more so than was anyone else
on the face of the earth."*
Numbers 12:3

Foreword

The figure of Moses towers over the cast of saints and sinners who fill the story of God's salvation in the Jewish Scriptures. He is the one chosen from birth to rebuild an enslaved people's faith in God, to persuade them to break from their masters, to win their freedom, to fight their battles against enemies, to find them food, to guide them in the wilderness, to persuade them to make covenant with their God, to teach them God's Torah, to help them learn wisdom in the spirit and to pacify God's anger against them when they sinned. No one in the biblical narrative ever played a more central role or bore more responsibility to carry out God's plan. And yet, the biblical testimonies to Moses might well surprise us. Given all that he is credited with doing, one would expect him to be described as a mighty warrior and resplendent leader as are judges like Gideon or kings like David and Solomon. But instead we find that almost everywhere Moses is remembered for his interior union with God, his spirituality of complete loyalty to God and his utter humility in accepting the tasks God assigned him.

Numbers 12:3–8, for example, opens with his own brother and sister, Aaron and Miriam, complaining about his leadership. Then the text pauses for a moment to reflect on this charge. It continues by describing Moses thus:

> Now the man Moses was very humble, more so than anyone else on the face of the earth. Suddenly the

LORD said to Moses, Aaron, and Miriam, "Come out, you three, to the tent of meeting...." And He said, "Hear my words: When there are prophets among you, I the Lord make myself known to them in visions; I speak to them in dreams. Not so with my servant Moses; he is entrusted with all my house. With him I speak face to face—clearly, not in riddles; and he beholds the form of the LORD."

Exodus 33 also describes Moses as the intimate soul-friend of God: Moses has just pleaded with God not to destroy the people who had made a Golden Calf as an idol even while Moses was receiving the Torah from God on the top of Sinai. In the midst of this, the author takes note that "Thus the Lord used to speak to Moses face to face, as one speaks to a friend" (Exod 33:11). It then continues with a remarkable dialogue between Moses and God:

Moses said to the LORD, "See, you have said to me, 'Bring up this people'; but you have not let me know whom you will send with me. Yet you have said, 'I know you by name, and you have also found favor in my sight.' Now if I have found favor in your sight, show me your ways, so that I may know you and find favor in your sight. Consider too that this nation is your people." He said, "My presence will go with you, and I will give you rest....I will do the very thing that you have asked; for you have found favor in my sight, and I know you by name." (Exod 33:12–17)

The final word on Moses in the Pentateuch echoes this view but gives us the one touch of glory and fame for God's hero. Moses has just died, and Deuteronomy observes:

> Never since has there arisen a prophet in Israel like Moses, whom the LORD knew face to face. He was unequaled for all the signs and wonders that the Lord sent him to perform in the land of Egypt, against Pharaoh and all his servants and his entire land, and for all the mighty deeds and all the terrifying displays of power that Moses performed in the sight of all Israel. (Deut 34:10–12)

These texts reflect the oldest view of Moses we possess that his heroic stature did not come primarily from his genius or his valor as a warrior, but from his particularly close relationship with God. Even one of the latest Jewish Wisdom works before the Common Era, the Book of Jesus ben Sirach, written about 180 B.C.E., reflects this tradition:

> For his faithfulness and meekness He consecrated him, choosing him out of all humankind. He allowed him to hear His voice, and led him into the dark cloud, and gave him the commandments face to face, the law of life and knowledge, so that he might teach Jacob the covenant, and Israel his decrees. (Sirach 45:4–5)

But Moses has been viewed through other lenses as well. Many Jewish commentators of the Talmudic era, whose reflections are found primarily in the targums, the midrashic texts and in the Talmud itself, heightened the miraculous accomplishments of Moses, often creating for his hidden years wonders and spectacular achievements (including becoming king of the Sudan) and accenting miracles that God performed to save him from danger in order to prepare him for his destined task of salvation. This was the natural development of national traditions that often develop around the founding father of a nation. Modern biblical scholars and historians have recovered much of the cultural background and many records of events of the second millennium, B.C.E., including the period in which the Exodus events took place. These literary remains and findings of archeology have often supported individual details of the cultural world of the biblical narratives. But because of the highly religious manner of presentation of the story that the Bible itself employs, secular historians often raise serious questions whether we can ever recover the actual historical facts. Whole books have been written that point out various presumed historical inaccuracies in the life of Moses. Although such works of professional historians are both legitimate and can throw light on difficult passages, they ultimately leave Jewish and Christian believers empty of inspiration and uncertain about the profound message of the Pentateuch as a masterpiece of faith. People have always looked to Moses as a model of fidelity to God. No wonder ancients speculated about the special favors God must have showered on his greatest servant. But without needing to create any further legends from the text, the authors of the Pentateuch propose a great truth for Israel's meditation: Namely that the person Moses represents all human beings in their spiritual struggle to be completely obedient to the word of God while wrestling with the meaning and value of their own destinies. From this point of view alone, the Exodus narrative's portrait of Moses deserves to be ranked among the greatest literary masterpieces of all time.

Joel Cohen has masterfully and sensitively captured just this insight into Moses in a new and fresh manner by imaging what it was like for Moses to look back over all the years of struggle with his own people, his destiny and his God. This book will help the reader rediscover the power of the drama of the Exodus anew, appreciate afresh the Bible's view of Moses and his accomplishment and provide a delightfully human touch to the sacred account of unprecedented divine action in history. To help all of us be enriched by the enormous body of traditions about Moses from which the author draws for his inner portrait of the man, he has included short excerpts and snapshots from a wide variety of older Jewish and early Christian literature that reveal the breadth of speculation and reflection that surrounded this greatest of biblical figures in every age, but especially in the formative centuries when the Hebrew Scriptures, the Christian Bible and the Talmudic literature were all being finalized as our foundational witness to God's revelation.

I believe everyone, Jew or Christian, who relaxes and enjoys this unique perspective, will come to understand the Scriptures more spiritually and with deepened faith.

Lawrence Boadt, C.S.P.

Preface

To the writer, the Books of Moses are Divine—truly, the word of God. They comprise a history that also describes the religious principles and laws of a people—but they are not a biography. The Books are laconic—they frequently leave, or intend, detail and nuance to the individual or collective imagination.

They identify critical events in the life of Moses, the primary figure in a people's history and religion. Still, the narration of many of those significant events is frequently contained in but a few words or sentences—nothing more. The details, the inner thinking of the human protagonists, were left on the cutting room floor of the Creator.

Some believe that key commentaries written hundreds or thousands of years later are part of an "oral tradition" transcendentally handed down generationally, in a process initiated by Moses himself. These commentaries explain, interpret and embellish on the people and events in the Bible, especially the leader Moses.

Those commentators, though, never lived through the events, nor interviewed Moses. They never gained direct insights from his contemporaries, nor researched the writings of his day—except the Bible. Theirs is truly an oral tradition.

The many volumes of the Bible and these commentaries explain Moses; but he never explains himself: What was *Moses* thinking? How did *Moses* perceive the events that surrounded and influenced him? Did Moses reflexively follow God's orders, or did he inwardly have second thoughts? Thus, have these many writers allowed Moses himself to tell his own story?

Some will feel strongly that it is mischievous, sacrilegious or even flatly heretical to study Moses' life, while disregarding these commentators. Some will see great arrogance in a concept that largely departs from these texts, and instead injects one's own thoughts into Moses' mind, during the hours of the Prophet left undescribed in the Bible. It might be, to them, still worse to memorialize these thoughts in a writing that audaciously tells the reader that they were purportedly authored by Moses—even a reader who recognizes the limitations of the exercise.

Those who will see defiance in the undertaking on either basis should read no further. Those, however, who perceive divinity for today in one's capacity to use the imagination to exercise one's belief in God, who seek cognition without the blinders of infallibility, are urged to continue.

For if continuing allows them to merely consider the author's perception of Moses, extrapolated onto him, then even reject the author's views as singularly unpersuasive or even vapid, and substitute their own views perhaps never uttered before, they will have made the process worthwhile.

They will have made Moses a truly *Living* Prophet.

Abbreviations

BaR	Medresh B'midbar Rabah
j. Sanhedrin	Tractate Sanhedrin from the Jerusalem Talmud
PR	Medresh Pisikta Rabosi
PRE	Pirkie Rabbi Eleazar
ShR	Medresh Shimos Rabah
Tan B	Medresh Tanchumah Hakdom V'Hayashan

Chapter 1
At Nebo

...[T]he LORD addressed Moses as follows: "Ascend this...Mount Nebo, which is in the land of Moab,...and view the land of Canaan, which I am giving to the Israelites for a possession; you shall die there on the mountain that you ascend...because...you broke faith with me among the Israelites at the waters of Meribath-kadesh in the wilderness of Zin, by failing to maintain my holiness among the Israelites. Although you may view the land from a distance, you shall not enter it—the land that I am giving to the Israelites."

(Deut 32:48–52)

I am about to die.

I suffer no illness nor frailty other than age. Yet, I walk in an unyielding, undeviating destiny.

My body is shriveled, my mind still clear. My Father walks beside me in my mind's eye, up and further up Mount Nebo, to a place that no one will ever visit, nor ever locate. My eyes are clear. I see unmistakably, as He has told me, what awaits me. My death, like my staff, is at hand. I can no longer hear the din of those left below.

I have lived six score. Excruciating as this climb is for me, He strangely commands me to climb onward to the site of my death. The heightening rock formation is unforgiving to my legs, as is the Almighty to my sin at the waters of Meribath. Life is a mountain; but there are no handgrips in sight to help me any longer.

Perhaps He merely tests me as He did Abraham before me, whom he directed to sacrifice his only son Isaac. Is there a reprieve that awaits me at the mountain's peak? For when Abraham passed his test, a ram caught in a thicket was there to be sacrificed to God in Isaac's stead. Will there be a ram caught in a thicket at Nebo to act as my substitute?

"He [Moses] was buried in a valley in the land of Moab, opposite Beth-peor, but no one knows his burial place to this day." (Deut 34:6)

Perhaps I hallucinate in the sharp, piercing rays of the midday sun. As I muse, the pounding of my heart and the words I speak in my mind reverberate. The pounding deafens me in the haunting stillness of the desert air. The quickening, blasting sheets of sand numb my face.

My sons will never know the place where He leads me. My children and all of the Israelites below and their descendants will never visit my tomb.

My faith is strong, but as my chest heaves with every added step, I suddenly fear in one trembling moment that I will be alone. I will be alone in death for Eternity— never allowed to enter the Land I covet.

The fear goes. It comes, and again is gone. Maybe it is simply the fear of a lonely man about to die, tormented by his inescapable fate.

I sin again in my weakness and my faithlessness. I sin by having come to covet, and by asking aloud why He plans my burial when there is no outward symptom, or physical need to die.

Does He lead me to this nowhere because the Israelites would otherwise create a shrine in my memory and come to worship at my gravesite, as they did the Golden Calf? This people, though, will not worship me—their frequent nemesis.

I ask to descend again to kiss my sons one last time. What kind of father am I to have left without an embrace to tell them that this is all just, and that life has been fair to me—and persuade them of my candor? But He turns me again, always up the mountain.

Some will later say that my anonymous gravesite is a testament to my humility. But the idea is His, not mine.

[Moses recalls:]
"At that time, too,
I entreated the
LORD, saying:
'O Lord God, you
have only begun to
show your servant
your greatness and
your might;...Let
me cross over to see
the good land
beyond the Jordan,
that good hill
country and the
Lebanon.' But the
LORD was angry
with me on your
account and would
not heed me. The
LORD said to me,
'Enough from you!
Never speak to
me of this matter
again! Go up to the
top of Pisgah and
look around you to
the west, to the
north, to the south,
and to the east.
Look well, for you
shall not cross over
this Jordan.'"
(Deut 3:23–27)

Only a short while back I was stopped in my climb, fixed in my tracks. His Book, curiously destined to bear my name, will not admit this lest the people come to repeat my doubting nature. Indeed, along this climb, I was a faithless, whining wretch.

I lowered my knees and begged Him once again. I could muster no tears this time. My tear ducts, too, were a desert. A sea of my tears had fallen, lost in the shifting sands of the desert. My eyes could summon tears no more. My parched throat disallowed my calling aloud to Him.

Still, I yearned so thoroughly for Him to hear my every thought. It was not a yearning for forgiveness for those I left below at the foot of the mountain range. It was not a prayer for a future generation that would honor His Ways even when faced with adversity. Nor did I seek a short respite to better teach Joshua to lead them.

No. There was no pretense of lofty purpose. It was a simple, selfish desire. I needed badly to reach and walk about the Land He promised to Abraham for us, so long ago. It would be better if He would deny me a teasing glimpse of the panorama that I will soon see from the mountaintop. Would Abraham have failed this test of his faith as I do now?

Still, were my sins so horrific? Did I rob? Did I covet women? Did I swear falsely? Was it that I struck a rock, instead of talking to it and, thus, I did not sanctify God to the Children of Israel? Was it that I lacked confidence when He commanded me to lecture Pharaoh, because I feared that my heavy tongue would show me as a fool? Indeed, He finds these sins mortal, more than my act of murdering the Egyptian taskmaster that He never punished.

Does He deny me my one desire, because the Land itself has become too important to me—that I showed no moderation in lusting after the tangible? Or, does He wish to teach the Israelites that they must undeviatingly follow the letter of His command? But, as my modesty wanes during my faith's ambivalence, I wonder if they will truly learn through the lesson. Or will they lose their faith, given what befell me?

The explanations I spew in my torment are in vain. My prophetic skills and dialogue with Him do not make this moment easier. My work is incomplete. My prophecy has achieved no reality for me in my lifetime.

He plans to show me the future. But there will be no future for me when my burial is complete. Am I the Moses that the Israelites would wish to deify, if only they knew my burial site?

In torment and in remembrance of things past, I throw my staff to the ground as I did in Pharaoh's palace. But the staff, the instrumentality of miracles against His enemies, is powerless against His will.

I am not sick. But I am about to die.

Chapter 2
Youth

The Egyptians became ruthless in imposing tasks on the Israelites, and made their lives bitter with hard service in mortar and brick and in every kind of field labor. They were ruthless in all the tasks that they imposed on them.

(Exod 1:13–14)

Then Pharaoh commanded all his people, "Every boy that is born to the Hebrews you shall throw into the Nile, but you shall let every girl live."

(Exod 1:22)

The daughter of Pharaoh came down to bathe at the river, while her attendants walked beside the river. She saw the basket among the reeds...she

*took him….She named him Moses, "because,"
she said, "I drew him out of the water."*

(Exod 2:5, 10)

*One day, after Moses had grown up, he went out
to his people and saw their forced labor. He saw
an Egyptian beating a Hebrew, one of his kins-
folk. He looked this way and that, and seeing no
one he killed the Egyptian and hid him in the
sand. When he went out the next day, he saw
two Hebrews fighting; and he said to the one
who was in the wrong, "Why do you strike your
fellow Hebrew?" He answered, "Who made you
a ruler and judge over us? Do you mean to kill
me as you killed the Egyptian?" Then Moses was
afraid and thought, "Surely the thing is known."
When Pharaoh heard of it, he sought to kill
Moses. But Moses fled from Pharaoh…."*

(Exod 2:11–15)

A cool breeze from below or above, from my past or from
my future, briefly soothes me. I rest for the moment against a
rock to prepare for the final ascent.

In my reverie, I see my life from the beginning. As I was
alone then, I am again now. Just as when an artist scratches off
the coloring of his portrait, he finds beneath an earlier portrait of

his subject—much the same, but the pain depicted in the subject's face is less wrinkled.

❦

I was too young to now remember how my sister Miriam looked after me from the river's edge, or from outside the palace gate even after I outgrew the gentle nursing of my true mother Jochebed. But in spite of their tendernesses to me, an aloneness hung over me all of my days. An aloneness foreseeable, explainable—unconquerable.

Only I among the Children of Israel avoided the humiliation of a slavery that Pharaoh was destined by God to impose on our people.

Pharaoh's daughter had rescued me at the river's edge. She adopted and pronounced me as her son, with no reservation. Her love was, for all to see, the complete love of a mother. She named me. She sheltered me. In her barren state, she defied her own father in love for me.

But Pharaoh saw me as simply a Hebrew who had escaped his edict. His deference was for his daughter, not me.

I walked the palace grounds in purple robe, treated as the grandson of a god. Indeed, in the eyes of Pharaoh's timid followers I was perchance a future god myself. But Pharaoh and his wise men

"[The angel tells Moses:] Afterwards, when you had grown up, you were brought to the daughter of Pharaoh and you became her son. But Amram, your [Israelite] father, taught you writing. And after you completed three weeks [of years, that is, twenty-one years], he brought you into the royal court."
(Jubilees 47:9)

8

knew better. They knew who I was. They knew what I was not, and would never be.

Outside the palace, my brothers and sisters, mud-covered in the brutal tar pit, heard the prideful murmurings of my mother and sister—that I was to be the Redeemer. But to these slaves and to myself I was nothing but a person who avoided the lash of the taskmaster and the misery of the tar pit. I was a "Redeemer" who never had to pay the tithe of hardship and pain that leaders must endure to warrant "leadership."

I was a lonely youth. I was a loner who traveled along the fault line between the worlds of master and slave—ever fearful of falling between the two, or fearful of even standing firmly on one side, or the other. I was a young man without an utterable past, resented both in the glory of the palace, and in the putre-fying tar pits at Pithom and Rameses; a young man resented by himself. Prophets, with His intercession, may be inspired to see the future; but this one is without capacity to unclog his past.

Was I a Hebrew, as Miriam had whispered in my ear, or a god, or as my "mother," Pharoah's daughter, told me? Were those condemned to the pits my brothers and sisters, or were they my servants, simply clothed in mud for their treachery? And why, as my princess "mother" would argue, should it mat-ter? I was her son, a prince—perhaps a god whose past was of no consequence.

My early years, thus, were never happy. I longed to be in the tar pits. Miriam's whispers deafeningly defined my being. I longed to lose my loneliness in that humiliation.

"Then the LORD said to Abram, 'Know this for certain, that your offspring shall be aliens in a land that is not theirs, and shall be slaves there, and they shall be oppressed for four hundred years; but I will bring judgment on the nation that they serve, and afterward they shall come out with great possessions.'" (Gen 15:13–14)

Looking back, I walked that day into the tar pits to lower myself into the pit of savagery and acknowledge the destiny spoken by him to our forefather, Abraham, four hundred years before, that our people would be aliens in a land not their own for four centuries. I would descend to the pits not as a "god" or a prophet, but as a Hebrew.

Would I have killed the taskmaster without a need to prove myself—to *me*? Did I kill merely to save another Hebrew's life at that moment? Did it matter to me whether the taskmaster was doing Pharaoh's command, or God's?

Or was I simply trying, in the only way I knew, to induce a personal suffering through my exile from the palace—by provoking Pharaoh to suffer me no longer? Perhaps, I killed to become a martyr—to escape from the triviality of being a "master," when *human* mastery was sinful. I heard from Miriam that all humans live in subjugation. Miriam's whispers told me that God was the only Master, and that Pharaoh only served the netherworld.

My killing of that nameless, faceless taskmaster was my reach for faith. While violence is not the way of His people, with that act, strangely, I became an Israelite. By it, I could turn back no longer across the Nile.

The killing was as it is described in His Book—nothing more, nothing less. It was a reckless act against an oppressor. I simply took revenge for my brother's subjugation into my own hands. In doing so I abandoned a tempered effort, first, to allay my brother's torture.

But no tortured explanation should be used to justify my own barbarity, however sincerely intended. Nor should it mitigate the violence I allowed myself when I exercised my free will that day across the Nile.

To do that, to defend "the Great Moses" and allow him to appear in memory to have acted "nobly," when he so offended God's law, would be a sin—perhaps as dreadful as the one I committed that day.

Pharaoh did not need to banish me thereafter. I needed to.

Chapter 3
The Fugitive

...He [Moses] settled in the land of Midian, and sat down by a well. The priest of Midian had seven daughters....Moses agreed to stay with the man, and he gave Moses his daughter Zipporah in marriage. She bore a son, and he named him Gershom; for he said, "I have been an alien residing in a foreign land."

(Exod 2:15–22)

I became a fugitive.

No mark emblazoned on my forehead would protect me from the warriors of an avenging Pharaoh, or the murmurs of my brothers wallowing in their misery. No mark to mitigate having so recklessly become "my brother's keeper." No City of Refuge from a guilty inner voice.

I bid farewell to no one. I longed to put my past to rest and to become a man without one. I abandoned along the wayside both my regal robe and my sister's fantasies. I looked across the desert sands for refuge. My eyes constantly searched back over my shoulder for revenge from Pharaoh—or from myself.

I began to cross the desert, armed only with the staff of a slave and the tattered garb of an exiled "prince of Egypt." By day, the blistering rays of the sun. By night, the painful cold. Both day and night, the blinding sandstorms and scorpions biting at my heel. They seemed the ingredients of an apothecary's mix to remedy a deeper wound. Physical pain became an antidote to inner turmoil.

The desert and its timeless meander, oddly, began to cleanse me within. The foolish daydreams of my enslaved sister Miriam, that I was the "Redeemer," were erased from my mind—an erasure enforced by the tyranny of the wilderness. By the end of my journey, I was, finally, at peace. I needed to look back no longer.

But although I did not see it then, an inevitable path still lay ahead. There is no detour, no circuitry, without a purpose.

The detour ahead, though—although it seemed, then, the inexorable causeway of my life—replenished me with the only true happiness in my lifetime. The Bible describes no happiness for me at any time, even along this detour. His Book is taut—no quarter for the superficial.

I arrived at the well near the tents of the Midianite Sheik Jethro. There, beside the well, I was drawn to a well of human kindness, Zipporah. She stupefied me with her dark-skinned beauty and dazzled me with her gracious spirit. What I now know as the Spirit of God reflected from her beautiful eyes, like the sun's rays bouncing off a clear spring.

She would walk with me, and love me for what I was, or appeared to be. She would ask me no questions. I would offer no answers. I was a man without a past or future—but she accepted me unconditionally. She watched me; and watched *over* me; and looked inside me. She never challenged me when my eyes surely told her that my mind had traveled to another time and place that would never be for me, or her. She accorded me cheerful humor—God's special solvent that protects us from the abrasions of life. She and the days at Midian became an oasis in the desert of my aloneness. Without a word to betray her silent thoughts, she intuited all that came before the well. She was, indeed, a prophet-in-reverse. I learned from her that for one to be a "prophet" does not require the title as such.

"[Jethro's] name was [also] Hobab [Num 10:20] because he loved the Torah, and amongst all the converts there was none who loved the Torah as Jethro did." (*Sifrei* Numbers 78)

Each day I would return at sunset from grazing her father's sheep, to see her body's silhouette against the tent. And when our son Gershom would playfully walk behind her as I approached, her tall form would cast a long shadow to shield him from the fiercely blinding rays of the sunset. The truly "protective" seem so effortless in protecting.

At night, we ate meat around the fire at a table prepared by Jethro, the only father that I ever knew. He serenaded us with his mandolin and with words of his trust in a "Universal God" who created the world: a God who has no enemies, except if they choose evil over good, and subjugate humans for their own purposes.

I courteously listened to him. But Jethro, I had heard from the passing caravans, had been a counselor to Pharaoh. The charming quality of the talks in which he urged me to partake was confusing and would lead my mind back across the desert to a place where, for me, there was no going back.

We exchanged gracious, unreserved smiles. Jethro, nonetheless, was a man at ease and harmony with himself, willing to bide his time. He projected a smile that seemed to say, with unremitting confidence: "There will come a day, my son. Your day."

Jethro would kiss me and the others good night. But as I tossed and turned beside Zipporah, his smile remained in my mind. Slumber would finally overcome his smile's knowing gesture. Smiles are fleeting, and the morning sun promised hard work and tiring repetitions for a shepherd. The sun would rise; the sheep would need to graze. And armed with Jethro's prayers, the sheep would be satisfied by day's end.

But I knew that the sheep in the flock of the Egyptian pagans would graze tomorrow, too. The sun would rise in Egypt across the desert. And the sheep in the flocks of Pharaoh, "the enemy of God," also would be satisfied.

Jethro spoke beautiful poetry. But I had heard poetry from the "bards" I left behind in the tar pits of Egypt. Poetry, I thought, merely squanders wondrous words, when the longings it speaks yield no redemption for those who suffer still.

Chapter 4
The Burning Bush

Moses was keeping the flock of his father-in-law Jethro, the priest of Midian; he led his flock beyond the wilderness, and came to Horeb, the mountain of God. There the angel of the LORD appeared to him in a flame of fire out of a bush; he looked, and the bush was blazing, yet it was not consumed. (Exod 3:1–2)

[God said:] "The cry of the Israelites has now come to me; I have also seen how the Egyptians oppress them. So come, I will send you to Pharaoh to bring my people, the Israelites, out of Egypt." But Moses said to God, "Who am I that I should go to Pharaoh, and bring the Israelites out of Egypt?" (Exod 3:9–11)

❦

*But Moses said to the L*ORD*, "O my Lord, I have*
never been eloquent, neither in the past nor even
now that you have spoken to your servant; but I
am slow of speech and slow of tongue." Then the
*L*ORD *said to him, "Who gives speech to mortals?*
Who makes them mute or deaf, seeing or blind?
*Is it not I, the L*ORD*?"*   (Exod 4:10–11)

*Then the anger of the L*ORD *was kindled against*
Moses....   (Exod 4:14)

Jethro's wondrous words thus were an argument, at odds
with what I consciously sought to banish from my memory. Truth,
inner truth, however, resists banishment.

❦

One day I walked the flock into the stillness of the desert,
planning, as every day, to bide my time alongside the grazing
flock, as Jethro would bide his, watching me graze on his words.

Although the Written Word records the events of that day,
it does not say that when I looked deep into that fire I saw for
myself His creation of the world, and all that came or would
come thereafter. His Book, with distinctive clearness, does not

reveal how I slapped my face while facing the glow of the fire, seeking return to the reality of my earthly chores.

At first, I was intrigued by it, but the vision refused to vanish. Was I immersed into a depthless dream? Was this the black magic of a diviner's apparition or a hallucination caused by one? Had the wine Zipporah prepared for me at sun-up turned sour in the heat of the day, and caused me ill effect? *Or did God appear to me?*

The glow persisted and would not subside. I needed to know whether what I saw was inside me or without me. Was it a conversion? Or had my inner eyes suddenly experienced a momentary sight of a longing maturing in the fire of my mind over my lifetime?

Did I see what I saw because He demanded that it be there to me? Or did I see it because I was inwardly searching for the outward sign of His arrival to deliver the enslaved from the tar pit?

Whichever it was, I will always know that no voice within a bush could alone have caused me to assume His mantle, or walk the path He urged upon me.

And while His anger flared in that moment of my stubbornness, I know that I could easily have caused the flame to disappear, through the double blink of an eye. The flame was there only for one willing to see it.

He imposed on me that day nothing I was unwilling to impose on myself. Despite His rage, I could easily have abandoned that moment and returned the flock to Jethro's gates without consequence. My will, then and always, was free.

Those who will be born across the Jordan will surely be free to ignore what has transpired in my lifetime. Their faith in God will not be buoyed by the miracles they simply read about in His Book. Nor does He ask that of them.

But why did His anger burn so that day for my "modesty" in resisting His call? Was it because someone already under His spell sought to evade him? Did He recognize that my modesty was simply a pretense to avoid commitment? Did He punish me from the fire because I should have shown greater adherence to Him? Does one's acceptance of God require greater bowing to His demand?

That exquisite fire expired; but, by the time the embers had died that afternoon, the sun, the moon and all the stars had already fallen upon me. There was no turning back. I had truly heard the Voice of God.

I was unprepared to return to the tent that night, nor for many nights ahead. I wandered in circles within the desert, not returning to camp until I knew that my eyes, or that my mind, had not betrayed me. I needed to be persuaded that I had not been seduced by a glorious caprice, come to lighten the load of a shepherd's burden.

When the Burning Bush stood inside me, when my faith had weathered the test of time, I returned to Zipporah to describe the story of my astonishment.

My life, as I had come to know it, was over. I had been resurrected from the living. I had no life purpose but to walk through the underworld, if it had to be. And I knew instantly that I would need to abandon the contentment I had come to cherish. Contentment was an implausible status for those whose siblings suffer so painfully. And I also knew, though He offered no clue of the resistance to follow, that the Israelites, themselves, would be hardest to persuade of God's plan.

Zipporah laughed when she heard my story. It was her last lighthearted moment. Rather than tarry to hear the detailed account of my full acceptance of the Lord, she began to pack our belongings for the road ahead.

Chapter 5
The Return

*Then the L*ORD *said to Abram, "Know this for certain, that your offspring shall be aliens in a land that is not theirs, and shall be slaves there, and they shall be oppressed for four hundred years; but I will bring judgment on the nation that they serve, and afterward they shall come out with great possessions.* (Gen 15:13–14)

*And the L*ORD *said to Moses, "When you go back to Egypt, see that you perform before Pharaoh all the wonders that I have put in your power; but I will harden his heart, so that he will not let the people go."* (Exod 4:21)

And he said, "Throw it on the ground." So he threw the staff on the ground, and it became a snake; and Moses drew back from it. Then the

LORD said to Moses, "Reach out your hand, and seize it by the tail"—so he reached out his hand and grasped it, and it became a staff in his hand—"so that they may believe that the LORD, the God of their ancestors, the God of Abraham, the God of Isaac, and the God of Jacob, has appeared to you." Again, the LORD said to him, "Put your hand inside your cloak." He put his hand into his cloak; and when he took it out, his hand was leprous, as white as snow. Then God said, "Put your hand back into your cloak"—so he put his hand back into his cloak, and when he took it out, it was restored like the rest of his body.   (Exod 4:3–12)

Afterward Moses and Aaron went to Pharaoh and said, "Thus says the LORD, the God of Israel, 'Let my people go, so that they may celebrate a festival to me in the wilderness.'" But Pharaoh said, "Who is the LORD, that I should heed him and let Israel go? I do not know the LORD, and I will not let Israel go." Then they said, "The God of the Hebrews has revealed himself to us; let us go a three days' journey into the wilderness to sacrifice to the LORD our God, or he will fall upon us with pestilence or sword…." That same day Pharaoh commanded the taskmasters of the people, as well as their

> *supervisors, "You shall no longer give the people*
> *straw to make bricks, as before; let them go and*
> *gather straw for themselves. But you shall*
> *require of them the same quantity of bricks as*
> *they have made previously...."*　　(Exod 5:1–8)

The outset of a lengthy journey often threatens the traveler with worry and frightening uncertainty. The identical journey from the perspective near a mountaintop depicts, instead, irresistible inevitability. The look back at circuitous paths, oppressive mountains and treacherous valleys—once foreboding are now straight and flattened. The impassable is now overcome. The fleeting promise of destiny is now replaced by an exquisite "providence."

It all seems so easy now. Our Liberation was a confluence of the destinies of "slave" and "master," even for those who did not worship God, nor even knew His name. God—indeed, the Creator even of Pharaoh who would ridicule me—declared our destinies to Abraham 350 years before I was born.

To be certain, God's miracles were used to persuade the Hebrews—not the Egyptians—of God's greatness. Indeed, Pharaoh could easily have been persuaded to "let my people go," through the prophecies of a latter-day Joseph called upon to interpret a disturbing dream for the pharaoh, as in days of old. But, we see that now, but didn't then.

As I hesitantly lumbered to the palace forty years ago, things were otherwise. I was surely pleased that God remembered His promise to liberate us, and by His assurance that the Pharaoh who would kill me had already died. And I was consoled by the strength of my brother Aaron who remained in Egypt, ever at my right arm along the trek.

But we were sweaty, bearded bedouins who climbed the palace staircase in the tattered garments of slavery. And, though, the Pharaoh who wanted to kill me was now dead, this Pharaoh knew that I was a disgraced runaway who had fled Egypt in cowardice, in the dark of night.

He, by contrast, was the Pharoah. He was a man, like his forefathers, schooled in the stiff-necked belief in his own divine right and infallibility. He was a descendent of rulers who took their possessions to their burial chambers to continue their dynasty in the hereafter.

His comely bearing befit him, and showed that Pharaoh was a warrior. He was a man whose manly muscles, though encased in perfumes and oils and metal bracelets, disclosed commitment to self-discipline. It was a commitment to endure the torture of inhuman plagues, if necessary—all to ensure mastery over his own people.

Pharaoh's veneer befit that of a "hero-god" that his people believed the Pharaoh to be. And with sinister affect he snickered at the halting approach of the displaced palace "prince" who returned from his exile, clad in the apparel and carriage of a beggar.

I could tell, at once, that my magician's tricks would be laughable to him and his court. For he was a ruler whose heart was hardened by God against the "strange men" to whom he granted an audience in order to cruelly entertain himself and his court.

But when Pharaoh mocked us when his necromancers easily imitated our "snake miracle," the converging destinies I now so easily see on history's roadmap were defined. Aaron and I became mired, instantly, in the quicksand of surrender.

We left in defeat. However, our defeat was inevitable. We had proposed to Pharaoh, simply, no reprisal, except the stated aspirations of an unnamed God. We bore no diplomat's portfolio, and tendered no compromise to move Pharaoh away from his imperious demeanor.

Man to man, even if the "man" Pharaoh believed that he was indeed a god, our demand was laughable.

We could hardly have argued that it was destiny of the Hebrews to be released, even if Pharaoh could understand what we truly meant by destiny. For the forecast of a fate of his doom is no more readily received by the high and mighty than a prediction of redemption is believed by the weak and demoralized.

Pharaoh's decision to reduce Aaron and me, the leaders of a seemingly foolish rebellion, to merchants of further agony for our followers by requiring that they not only lay the bricks but also make them was predictable. It was, also, perhaps, a brief sojourn that the Hebrews simply misperceived at the time, along the road to what was truly our "Destiny."

Chapter 6
The Ten Plagues

"So I will stretch out my hand and strike Egypt with all my wonders that I will perform in it; after that he will let you go." (Exod 3:20)

Then Moses answered, "But suppose they do not believe me or listen to me, but say, 'The LORD did not appear to you.'" (Exod 4:1)

...[H]e lifted up the staff and struck the water in the river, and all the water in the river was turned into blood,....But the magicians of Egypt did the same by their secret arts.

(Exod 7:20, 22)

The LORD did so, and great swarms of flies came into the house of Pharaoh and into his officials' houses; in all of Egypt the land was ruined because of the flies. (Exod 8:24)

At midnight the LORD struck down all the firstborn in the land of Egypt, from the firstborn of Pharaoh who sat on his throne to the firstborn of the prisoner who was in the dungeon, and all the firstborn of the livestock. Pharaoh arose in the night, he and all his officials and all the Egyptians; and there was a loud cry in Egypt, for there was not a house without someone dead.

(Exod 12:29–30)

The story of the Exodus is not told in the style of a gifted storyteller.

God's narration does not transport the listener to the mind or body of those who truly observed His miracles. His Writing does not allow the blind to see what came before. His story, flatly written, contains lessons for the generations to follow. But it allows one's imagination to remain one's own. One's beliefs as to the existence of the "miraculous" remain one's own, and are not forced upon the reader.

Those who wish to remain blind or deaf are not compelled either to see or hear. They are never overborne by an overpowering account. Aaron and I were simply instructed to stretch out our arms and staffs, and the miracles that God predicted came, and later went.

"If you refuse to let them go, I will plague your whole country with frogs."
(Exod 8:2)

There is no deafening sound of croaking frogs, leaping into every crevice of Egyptian life. Nor is there a vivid depiction of gripping fright borne of wild animals terrorizing people and cattle, in field and home. We feel no omnipresent boils torturing even Pharaoh's wise men, body and soul. Nor do we read of an enveloping rapture with which a thick, impenetrable darkness later blinded the sighted to believe that they would never see again.

And, finally, there are no excruciating cries and screeches, eerie enough to cause the listener to cry with empathy, as a mist and mass of death spreads across Egypt, as God declares his vengeance.

Instead, simple sentences describe a year's on-again, off-again agony inflicted on our enemy.

Are these flat descriptions of miracles a testament to "free will"—that would be unachievable if the account were too graphic?

The lesson is that miracles exist only for those who allow themselves to observe them, or are willing to accept them. Only true belief, not well-sculpted stories, allows miracles to be perceived. Indeed, even having observed the miracles that defeated Pharaoh, the Israelites so often lost faith once they arrived in the desert.

Was it that the Israelites saw God as changeable? Did they fear that He would not again come to their aid, and save them from annihilation, or thirst, or faithlessness? Or did they simply take His miracles for granted?

I stand against this rock and wonder what tomorrow brings—things not known to us today, or even conjured or imagined. Will these things that I imagine to be miracles today be taken for granted tomorrow or many years from now?

Our descendants may, indeed, ask how the Israelites of my day were so faithless, given the miracles in Egypt, at the Red Sea or in the Wilderness. But will those who confront my brothers' and sisters' shortcomings not be wrongful to them in making their accusations?

Conjure, for example, things that are miracles or apparitions today—but maybe not so tomorrow.

Man, like the eagle, might someday fly. Perhaps tomorrow's wise men, imbued with the spirit of God, could create a device that would have allowed us to rise into the air in chariots to escape Pharaoh's army. Might there someday be a device to defy the force that causes humans to cling to the ground?

Would such device be less miraculous tomorrow than that which we observed in Egypt? Would it not suffice to prove His greatness and compel faithfulness in the deserts of tomorrow?

Or, someday our wise men may acquire sufficient wisdom to replenish lost blood, such as that of our brothers defeated by our savage enemy Amalek. Would they be able to use the healthy blood of their sons and daughters? And if so, should they not see it as a miracle?

Or some night in the generations to follow, when the moon is full, our descendants may perhaps look heavenward knowing that a man has reached the moon. And if so, should they not see it as a miracle?

Or someday there may be a device that, in our day, could have listened and watched as Aaron and I stood before Pharaoh and told him Egypt's fate if he did not release us? Might there, someday, be a device that would have allowed Israelites and Egyptians alike seeming presence in Pharaoh's palace? And if so, should they not see it as a miracle?

These thoughts that I conjure might be "miracles" even greater than those He performed in the year of our Liberation. And if they come into being will our children nonetheless not see them as miracles that prove God's existence? Will they take them for granted instead and reduce them to the "ordinary"? Like the rising sun. Or the waning moon. Or a child being born.

Chapter 7
The Sea of Reeds

When Pharaoh let the people go, God did not lead them by way of the land of the Philistines, although that was nearer; for God thought, "If the people face war, they may change their minds and return to Egypt." So God led the people by the roundabout way of the wilderness toward the Red Sea. (Exod 13:17–18)

Then the LORD said to Moses: Tell the Israelites to turn back and camp…by the sea. Pharaoh will say of the Israelites, "They are wandering aimlessly in the land; the wilderness has closed in on them." I will harden Pharaoh's heart, and he will pursue them, so that I will gain glory for myself over Pharaoh and all his army; and the Egyptians shall know that I am the LORD. And they did so. (Exod 14:1–4)

The LORD hardened the heart of Pharaoh king of Egypt and he pursued the Israelites....The Egyptians pursued them, all Pharaoh's horses and chariots, his chariot drivers and his army....
(Exod 14:8–9)

Then Moses stretched out his hand over the sea. The LORD drove the sea back by a strong east wind all night, and turned the sea into dry land; and the waters were divided. The Israelites went into the sea on dry ground, the waters forming a wall for them on their right and on their left. The Egyptians pursued, and went into the sea after them, all of Pharaoh's horses, chariots, and chariot drivers.
(Exod 14:21–23)

Then the LORD said to Moses, "Stretch out your hand over the sea, so that the water may come back upon the Egyptians, upon their chariots and chariot drivers." So Moses stretched out his hand over the sea, and at dawn the sea returned to its normal depth. As the Egyptians fled before it, the LORD tossed the Egyptians into the sea.
(Exod 14:26–27)

"But not alone the adults took part in this song, even the sucklings dropped their mothers' breasts to join in singing; yea, even the embryos in the womb joined the melody, and the angels' voices swelled the song. God so distinguished Israel during the passage through the Red Sea, that even the children beheld His glory, yea, even the woman slave saw more of the presence of God by the Red Sea than the Prophet Ezekiel was ever permitted to behold." (Mekilta Shitah 1, 35a; Tehillim 8, 77; Sotah Tosefta 6.4; Legends III)

We strode with great force, beginning in the dead of night.

The cadence of our march and the prideful hymns that we sang belied the clanging of blood-stained chains that still encased the bruised and broken ankles of our legions. But we had been liberated, and nothing could change that. Nothing could reverse an exodus from torture, slavery and humiliation. We were released from the will of idol worshippers and their own idol that had subjugated God's people. God's miracles had crushed the collective will of our oppressors.

Our time of terror was unalterably behind us, for He had promised us so. Pharaoh had even been dealt the loss of his own firstborn, when the Midnight Caller Himself made Pharaoh and his followers see the light. So we brimmed with the hope of an undoable salvation.

But, curiously, He marched us roundabout to a place that would seem to leave no escape from a new plight. Speedily, we strode, even on hobbled legs. And although He paraded us away from the Philistine canyons to protect us from our own doubts, He took us directly to the Sea: a place that would allow "no retreat." It was a waterlocked edge of the world, for proceeding forward would push us into the water despite the seeming strength of our conviction.

So in "protecting" us from our own doubts, He mysteriously walked us directly into doubt. With an awakening, cold slap at Pharaoh's face, God reminded him that his slaves had left in final liberation. But, it was not enough for God to remind Pharaoh. So, again, He strengthened Pharaoh's heart to not let go his precious slaves. And, thusly, He compelled Pharaoh to pursue us through the wilderness and then directly to the Sea.

They kept coming on the dry land. We, our crooked bodies, faced the sea. They, in contrast, rode gleaming chariots, laughing at the swirling dust we left behind as their speeding wheels overtook us.

Pharaoh was no longer the defeated, fatherless, hero-god of three days before. Once again, he was the dauntless conqueror, to whom defeat was unthinkable and impossible. We, though, once more, were reduced to slaves, again awaiting impending defeat at Pharaoh's hands. The certainty of our death, either in the bottomless sea before us or under the horses of Pharaoh galloping behind, replaced the certainty of His promise.

To be sure, He had a plan in mind. And that plan, in one exalted moment, would gather in the confidence of one zealot: A single man would stride boldly into the sea and risk drowning himself in a "leap of faith" unknown to the Children of Israel since Abraham.

It was the fidelity of Nahshon, son of Aminadov, the Lion of Judah. He, like the rest of us, was unable to swim or even float.

But he risked life itself by walking directly into the Sea even up to his chin, when the moment of truth was at hand. It was Nahshon alone who refused to hesitate at the water's edge. Nahshon's faith, not my outstretched arm, parted the waters.

But Nahshon was a single man who stood as a tall statue in the desert. God could not have considered the constancy of Nahshon's faith as typical. His was not a faith that would be repeated in all his Israelite peers.

To many, God's actions here seemed to undermine his goal to rescue us from despair while en route to the Promised Land. For truly, He substituted the army of the Philistines with the oncoming chariots of Pharaoh's militia. And Pharaoh's attack was curiously incited by God Himself to chase us to the Sea.

But God knew, as only He is able, that true redemption of man's spirit sometimes will require not only bodily and spiritual withdrawal from subjugation—but also a withdrawal that could never be undone. He knew that if we faced a confrontation at the canyons of the Philistines three short days from Egypt, even a victory would have left His people in despair. For surely they would have envisioned future carnage. An instant return to Egypt would have seemed, to them, the path of least resistance.

But a victory spawned in a "miracle" would be different. A miracle would show not only the value of "faith" such as Nahshon's, but also make the redemption complete. It would not only glorify God, but also break the slavemind's capacity to undo the course that God had chosen.

Once the walls of water came crashing down after our safe passage, the Israelites could no longer return to Egypt, however much they were provoked. We may surely have retreated from the Philistines hosts, either in victory or defeat. But we could never turn back once a miracle erased the pathway of a retreat.

"Redemption" sometimes requires the removal of free will. The crashing walls of the Sea of Reeds, even more than their miraculous construction, were proof of His glory. By His miraculous design, the redemption would become undoable. The genius of His design would be a proof of God's magnificence, even greater than the miracle of a parted sea.

Chapter 8
The Decalogue

On the third new moon after the Israelites had gone out of the land of Egypt, on that very day, they came into the wilderness of Sinai. They had journeyed from Rephidim, entered the wilderness of Sinai, and camped in the wilderness; Israel camped there in front of the mountain. Then Moses went up to God; the LORD called to him from the mountain, saying, "Thus you shall say to the house of Jacob, and tell the Israelites: You have seen what I did to the Egyptians, and how I bore you on eagles' wings and brought you to myself. Now therefore, if you obey my voice and keep my covenant, you shall be my treasured possession out of all the peoples. Indeed, the whole earth is mine."

(Exod 19:1–5)

So Moses came, summoned the elders of the people, and set before them all these words that the LORD had commanded him. The people all answered as one: "Everything that the LORD has spoken we will do."   (Exod 19:7–8)

The LORD heard your words when you spoke to me, and the LORD said to me: "I have heard the words of this people, which they have spoken to you; they are right in all that they have spoken. If only they had such a mind as this, to fear me and to keep all my commandments always, so that it might go well with them and with their children forever! Go say to them, 'Return to your tents.' But you, stand here by me, and I will tell you all the commandments, the statutes and the ordinances, that you shall teach them, so that they may do them in the land that I am giving them to possess."   (Deut 5:28–31)

When the LORD descended upon Mount Sinai, to the top of the mountain, the LORD summoned Moses to the top of the mountain, and Moses went up. Then the LORD said to Moses, "Go down and warn the people not to break through to the LORD to look; otherwise many of them will

*perish. Even the priests who approach the LORD
must consecrate themselves or the LORD will
break out against them."*   (Exod 19:20–22)

*Then God spoke all these words: "I am the LORD
your God, who brought you out of the land of
Egypt, out of the house of slavery...."*
(Exodus 20:1–2)

The morning sun burned off many of its clouds. Sinai began
to take shape in front of us—but we could not see through the
remaining clouds to its pinnacle. Unlike Nebo, Sinai was a mountain whose highest peak I did, indeed, wished to conquer.

Throughout my life as a leader, I would always be mired in
quicksand. Perhaps these shortcomings were why I always saw
my *true* calling as a teacher. I would come, thus, to see my role
atop Sinai as removing the overcast that had left the Israelites in
a darkened faithlessness during the seven weeks of travel from
Egypt. For thrice they had stumbled and lost faith at the Sea of
Reeds, at the Wilderness of Sin where they complained of famine
and at Rephidim where they complained of thirst. God indeed
saved them time and again from drowning, hunger and thirst.

These dramatic signs made it odd to me at Sinai that Israel
could, so filled with excitement, plan for this great moment in our
history. I was truly astonished that they could so easily affirm that
"everything that God has spoken we shall do"—even before He
stated His demands atop the Mountain.

Was the ardor of this vow (so soon later abandoned) borne slowly, but inevitably in a purifying process that had lasted four hundred years? Indeed, was it the extended humiliation that allowed us to "leap" to accept the Torah—even though, as we came to understand, each nation, too stiff-necked to succumb to God, had already, we were told, declined the Torah? Was our "chosen" status derived from the reality that all the others had already eliminated themselves?

It almost seemed that if He required each Israelite to murder his son, they would, in a moment of zealotry, have accepted that obligation as well. Were there, as it seemed at that instant, 600,000 Abrahams poised at Sinai's base to await my return?

Given their frequent stumblings en route from Egypt, I should, in truth, have begun the Feast of the New Moon in the third month, which fell on the sixth day of the month of Sivan, with concern. In truth, though, the morning's optimism knew no bounds. Destiny was at hand for all of the world, and we were chosen as messengers for it all. And, we believed, in some way, that we were messengers for all our children that

"[At the conclusion of the creation:] He [God] said to us [angels]: 'I will now separate off a people for Myself from among My nations. They too will keep the Sabbath. I will make the people holy to Me, and I will bless them, just as I [blessed and] made holy the Sabbath day. I will make them holy to Me [and] in this way I will bless them: they will become My people and I will be their God. I have chosen [for this role] the sons of Jacob among all of those whom I have seen. I have recorded them as my firstborn son and have made them holy to Me throughout the ages of eternity." (Jubilees 2:19–20)

would ever be. To us, all the unborn or even yet to be conceived, in some form, stood silently beside the Mountain that morning.

This was, however, a vision of God that I would largely experience alone. For the Israelites petrified by the thunder, lightning and piercing sound of the ram's horn could not accept the starkness or intensity of His rapture. They implored me to receive it alone for them.

Surely, it was important that they, too, hear at least the beginning of His Decalogue, lest they come to conclude that having ascended alone, I had become a hermit. I feared that they would see me as a man inspired only by his own imagination: a man who himself had authored the Sacred Code engraved on tablets, with which he would later return from a mystery-shrouded mountaintop.

Did God, however, intend my solitary receipt of the Torah to enable them to disavow His Commandments? For if they had directly received all of His Commandments as did I, to defy His Ways would have been unimaginable. Did He, then, intend His appearance that morning to be so awful to them in order to accord them "free will"? My solitary ascent surely contributed to their withdrawal from the Covenant just forty days later. How could anyone who actually saw or heard what I alone saw and heard have so easily rejected Him later?

But to turn to that day's occurrences—God had spoken to me before, beginning at the Burning Bush. Aaron, too, had heard the Voice when God spoke to us together. Still, Aaron and I never discussed these haunting moments. Aaron's eyes and mine simply met to help allay the fears that stirred within us, that, perchance, we had been consumed by the occult, not the Divine.

Before the arrival at Sinai, for fear of uprising or rebuke or hostile laughter, Aaron and I would never describe to the Israelites what it was like to hear the Voice of God. Always, unable or afraid, we would imply that responding to the question would lead to "Sacred Ground," such as at the Burning Bush. It was a place, like the ineffable name of God, not fit for saying aloud.

I would never, again, after the sixth of Sivan, be asked about the Voice. Until that morning I myself, even though allied in the experience with my Aaron, was never truly certain of what I had heard, because even though I had heard it, I could not recount it, nor receive affirmation of it from others. Looking back, now, I could not bring myself to confide its beauty even to Zipporah, from whom there were no other secrets. Did the Voice of God alienate me even from my God-fearing wife, whom I loved too with all my heart?

Until that morning the Voice was somewhat like the sound one would hear of one's own voice while standing in a mountain canyon—speaking aloud, fingers tightly glued into one's ears saying: *"I am the LORD your God."* I would hear the eerie sound, but no words would come from my mouth, no fingers would be pressed within my ears. I am unsure even now if I heard the Voice from within, or from without.

Still, the nodding agreement of Aaron allowed me to know that I had not gone mad. Faith finds safety in the affirmation by others of one's own belief. Oh so great must have been the faith of Abraham to have believed so firmly, despite his initial aloneness in it. Abraham was truly a Lonely Man of Faith—the aloneness in his faith perhaps greater than anything else for which he stood. I wonder often if Abraham, like me, sometimes stood in the dark desert night peering at the moon, his pressed fingers within his ears to "rehear" the Voice, and utter to himself the words: *"Hear O Israel the LORD, our God, the LORD is One."*

In the days before, the people sanctified themselves, abandoning sensual delight not appropriate at Sinai. As we each gazed toward the Mountain, we could see that the day would be like no other. The Mountain, which before had been like any other mountain, was suddenly encased in thunder and lightning, fire and smoke. It was, for all to see, a calamity of His Revelation.

The people, at first, were so energized that He needed to warn them not to rush toward the Mountain to embrace it. Suddenly, though, they were retreating, terrorized. Thousands recoiled in terror—pulling their shawls above their heads in despair. Many fell upon their children to shield them from harm's way.

It seemed as if a midday sun had suddenly pierced through directly to the earth's center: a site that had been in perpetual darkness since the Second Day of Creation, when the people had crawled out of the cave into a never-seen sunlight. The Israelites' fear that day was, without question in my mind, the way in which God wanted the people to fear Him.

So although I had already ascended the Mountain on the prior two days to hear His preliminary edicts, this day's Voice was different. And although the people recoiled as I rose from the base of the Mountain, they did truly see me walk into the furnace at its peak.

"The LORD spoke with you face to face at the mountain, out of the fire. (At that time I was stand-ing between the LORD and you to declare to you the words of the LORD; for you were afraid because of the fire and did not go up the moun-tain.) And he said: I am the LORD your God…" (Deut 5:4–6)

No longer was it only Aaron and I that heard His Voice, and no longer were we isolated zealots. My reactions could now surely be seen by the Israelites. For now, they began to *"know,"* just as surely as did Aaron and I, that my ascent was des-tined to hear the Voice of God.

So—I reached my station that would protect them, having left Aaron and the priests below. God, then, told me to descend again and warn those below, even the priests, who might try to burst through to see Him. But as I walked back down, they were all turned away in seeming retreat from God's Holy Spirit.

I nonetheless cried out a warning to them. The sound of my words bounced off the surrounding mountains for them to hear.

In unison they nodded in fealty to His directive. But the sound they would hear immediately changed. It lasted for an "instant" that would last an eternity: *"I am the* LORD *your God, who brought you out of the land of Egypt, out of the house of slavery; you shall have no other gods before me. You shall not make for yourself an idol, whether in the form of anything that is in heaven above, or that is on the earth beneath, or that is in the water under the earth."* (Exod 20:2–4)

"When all the people witnessed the thunder and lightning, the sound of the trumpet, and the mountain smoking, they were afraid and trembled and stood at a distance, and said to Moses, 'You speak to us, and we will listen; but do not let God speak to us, or we will die.'" (Exod 20:18–19)

No Israelite in that brief, painful moment uttered a discernible word. Still, I could hear the painful, wrenching cries of the Assembly, unable to bear it any longer. Aaron stood beside me. Ever their protector, he pulled at my cloak, even at this instant that required our total commitment. He wanted to show me the torture that brought the frightened people to their knees. Then, in one alarming cry, they begged me to ascend again instantly: "Go up, and hear His Voice alone, for we will die." I could no longer abide their shrieks. I relented and ascended, intending later to repeat to them the words I would hear upon the Mountain.

The Voice that I now heard atop the Mountain had a different quality than before. He preached to me the remainder of the Ten Pronouncements. These words I would repeat to the Israelites before night fell that day. The different sound, though, was because it now revealed the sound of His satisfaction as a teacher.

❧

I stood there silently, having left Aaron, his sons Nadav and Abihu and the seventy Elders below. I listened intently to concentrate on God's every word, not seeing or hearing anything else. I knew that my task was to repeat word for word for the Israelites below the remaining Eight Commandments. But I was, and would be during the forty days to follow, as in a trance—focused on the only thing that there was for me: His Voice.

I would not act now as an interpreter. These words required no interpretation and yielded, despite their splendor, no surprises. My role would be more like that of a funnel that stood upside down. God would pour His Commandments through the narrow cylinder of my voice, to be showered upon the Israelites.

Surely there would be nuance to these Commandments— Does one commit adultery by simply lusting in one's heart? Does one violate the Sabbath when he hammers a rock that cannot be broken? Does one rob when he takes what belongs to him? But the Israelites would need no interpretation for "why" those rules were necessary. The positive Commandments spoke eloquently for themselves. Nor could one misunderstand their momentousness, or require explanations for the prohibitions. My role was simply to pass on His words.

While amidst the Mountaintop, I tried to hide inside me a brief irreverent smile. It revealed that I no longer suffered from the shame of the stammerer. I recognized that my ploy to evade

His command at the Burning Bush was nothing more than that—a ploy invoked by a reluctant man who lacked enough faith.

These moments atop Sinai, as He spoke the last Eight Commandments, thus, were fast fleeting. I would not need to scratch my head, nor pull at my whiskers, nor squint into the distance to help better understand their meaning. Even a nonbeliever could surely have recognized that these Commandments were not unclear. Nor did they require the genius of the Almighty.

The frightening sound of the Voice was, thus, perhaps more to remind us that, while these were laws that any society needed, we needed them simply because He demanded it—even though they were guideposts steeped in common sense and the needs of the Congregation. So, in some strange way, every law He gave, no matter how logical for a society, was really a command based not on logic or reason but on belief. It is obeyed simply because God commanded it, and nothing more. So, in fact, many of the laws I received from God did not come with explanations—such as the law concerning what we may eat or may not eat.

"When Gentiles, who do not possess the law [the Torah], do instinctively what the law requires, these, though not having the law, are a law to themselves. They show that what the law requires is written on their hearts, to which their own conscience also bears witness; and their conflicting thoughts will accuse or perhaps excuse them..."
(Rom 2:14–15)

As I look back on these moments before my descent, though I trembled, I was truly happy. It was a happiness, though, that I only savor in looking back. Happiness, to quote the cynic, is something one remembers, not that one experiences. I was too fearful, responsible and engaged to be happy, then.

I descended and briefly met with the Elders and the Priests. Rather than allow time to elapse and, thus, forget what I had learned, I strode directly to the camp, where silence abounded. I immediately repeated His words. So focused was I on the duties to narrate, I closed my eyes throughout it. When my task was complete, I opened my eyes to observe the nodding willingness of every Israelite—even unto the rear of the assembly.

I peered closely to ensure myself that what He had asked was not too hard: what I had observed of their faithlessness at the Wildernesses of Sin, the Sea of Reeds and Rephidim was in the distant past. His radiance shone on the face of every Israelite. I harbored pity for all the desert heathens whom we would meet. For by dint of arrogance, they had squandered their chance at His love.

But there was no time to collect memories. I was obliged to teach them the law to guide the conduct among men. I had to return to the Mountaintop to receive the Israelites' destiny, to which they had decisively committed themselves.

The midday sun now stood directly above us: the hour when the worshippers of the Egyptian sun god, *Amon Ra,* would religiously pay it homage. But for us, it was an hour that God had chosen for another purpose: to begin to teach the laws stating the Israelite's duties to his fellow. It was a code of conduct that pays heed to God, not his creations.

"Now when Moses wished to proceed to the selection of the seventy elders, he was in a sore predicament because he could not evenly divide the number seventy among the twelve tribes, and was anxious to show no partiality to one tribe over another, which would lead to dissatisfaction among Israel. Bezalel, son of Uri, however, gave Moses good advice. He took seventy slips of paper on which was written 'elder,' and with them two blank slips, and mixed all these in an urn."
(Keneset Israel [1885], 309, seq., Legends III)

I sat at the base of the Mountain surrounded by the seventy Elders. There was silence in the camp. The thunder and lightning and shrill sound of the ram's horn had already abated. Again, the Voice appeared; but, now, more tender than before. It was not so haunting or thunderous; it allowed me to receive and immediately recite for all the Israelites the words I would hear. These words came in short, clear sentences that I, in turn, taught to the people.

There was no interpretation nor nuance nor method. While there would come a time to describe their spirituality, the Voice described only the letter of His laws. I looked out upon the Congregation as I repeated the words I heard. And I saw, again, the steady, nodding agreement of the Congregation. It pleased me greatly.

As I continued, I came to where He told me, and I them: *"When people who are fighting injure a pregnant woman so that there is a miscarriage, and yet no further harm follows, the one responsible shall be fined what the woman's husband demands, paying as much as the judges determine. If any harm follows, then you shall give life for life, eye for eye, tooth for tooth, hand for hand, foot for foot, burn for burn, wound for wound, stripe for stripe."* (Exod 21:22–25)

I looked quickly beyond the Elders to the masses who gathered to see the nodding continue uninterrupted. They were not surprised to hear words suggesting a "principle" of seeming brutality, a law of equal punishment, imposed on the Congregation. For they had just ascended from the Land of Pharaoh, for whom savagery was the manner of life. The slavery that had spanned the people's lifetime made it seem that any civilization would tolerate savagery. The Israelites well knew that a slave who even injured another "possession" of Pharaoh would himself be killed. Why should such retribution not exist here as well, like in the laws of Pharaoh in Egypt or of Hammurabi, the famous king of Babylon?

"Seventy-two elders, six to each tribe, now advance and each drew a slip. Those whose slips were marked 'elder' were elected, while those who had drawn blank slips were rejected, but in such a wise that they could not well accuse Moses of partiality." (Keneset Israel [1885], 309, seq., Legends III)

My eyes, however, focused on the Elders, who expected more humanity in God's judgments. I perceived the trouble in their eyes when first they heard the simple phrase: *"an eye for an eye,"* and the words that followed. I saw in them a fear that God's "civilization" might repeat the barbarity of Egypt.

I smiled, briefly, calming them with a gesture of my outstretched hand. For I knew that the letter of the law they heard that afternoon merely stated the framework of His command. Thus, with just a halting gesture of my hand, I persuaded the Elders that on the morrow I would begin to learn—to later teach them and, they, in turn, the Congregation—the Oral Torah that would make clear and polished the sometimes, difficult to comprehend. It would be a tradition to bring the qualities of mercy

"The proposal [concerning the coming famine and how to head it off] pleased Pharaoh and all his servants. Pharaoh said to his servants, 'Can we find anyone else like this—one in whom is the spirit of God?' So Pharaoh said to Joseph, 'Since God has shown you all this, there is no one so discerning and wise as you. You shall be over my house, and all my people shall order themselves as you command; only with regard to the throne will I be greater than you.'"
(Gen 41:37–40)

and of reason to His law. It would make understandable to the Congregation laws frequently too harsh and unintended if studied too strictly.

Once the Elders recognized that the days ahead would allay their concerns, a smile emerged—across their faces. And in turn it would show across the faces of the Congregation.

When I completed repeating His ordinances I handwrote all the words God had uttered. Exhausted, together with the Congregation I said the evening prayer, as on no other day of my life. I walked to my tent and warmly embraced Zipporah and our sons. I lay down to sleep, without a word spoken. It would be the last night I would sleep for forty days.

I dreamed, that night, that I had ascended, and heard the Voice of God at Sinai. Dreams, Joseph, son of Jacob, told us long ago, such as when he interpreted Pharaoh's own dreams, may come true. But dreams, or even nightmares, are fleeting. Reality is what stands the test of time.

Chapter 9
Atop Sinai

*And Moses wrote down all the words of the
LORD. He rose early in the morning, and built an
altar at the foot of the mountain, and set up
twelve pillars, corresponding to the twelve tribes
of Israel. He sent young men of the people of
Israel, who offered burnt offerings and sacrificed oxen as offerings of well-being to the LORD.
Moses took half of the blood and put it in basins,
and half of the blood he dashed against the altar.
Then he took the book of the covenant, and read
it in the hearing of the people; and they said, "All
that the LORD has spoken we will do, and we will
be obedient." Moses took the blood and dashed it
on the people, and said, "See the blood of the
covenant that the LORD has made with you in
accordance with all these words."*

(Exod 24:4–8)

❧

Then Moses went up on the mountain, and the cloud covered the mountain. The glory of the LORD settled on Mount Sinai, and the cloud covered it for six days; on the seventh day he called to Moses out of the cloud. Now the appearance of the glory of the LORD was like a devouring fire on the top of the mountain in the sight of the people of Israel. Moses entered the cloud....

(Exod 24:15–18)

When I [Moses] went up the mountain to receive the stone tablets, the tablets of the covenant that the LORD made with you, I remained on the mountain forty days and forty nights; I neither ate bread nor drank water. And the LORD gave me the two stone tablets written with the finger of God; on them were all the words that the LORD had spoken to you at the mountain out of the fire on the day of the assembly.

(Deut 9:9–10)

On the seventh of Sivan, I would climb higher toward the heaven, some Elders would say, than any man. It was to a place far above where the smoke from the sacrificial altar would flatten. It was to a height that would confirm that any sacrifice to God, was nothing more than a meager undertaking.

First, I stood among the Elders watching the smoke rise as the youths sacrificed the bulls. I wondered whether the Israelites fully grasped what was at issue at the quickly made altars at Sinai's base, and feared that our descendants might see savagery in this act of dedication. And I thought that perhaps someday, like human sacrifice in the culture of other peoples, animal sacrifice would be replaced. Might not acts of charity or the sacrifice of human pleasures, if authorized by God, prove to be better signs of one's devotion?

But this slave people needed the hard and fast to remind them that, like the slaughtered bulls atop the altars, we had little choice in our destiny without God's intervention. For we were, finally, no more free than Isaac, who was released from his altar only by God's intercession. Thus, the bull's blood that I sprinkled that morning would, unforgettably, symbolize to the Israelites their *own* blood: They were spared from death by the bulls offered in direct substitution for them. The blood, still, seemed a primitive gesture to me. I hoped, though, that the sprinkling blood would graphically depict for them, especially the sinner, life's utter tenuousness.

But bloodstains become dulled over time, like the Voice of God. Will the seemingly "primitive" be an effective form of worship tomorrow, when it proved so futile at Sinai so soon after God revealed Himself? And will the generations reject it, or will our enemies compel its rejection by conquering us and defiling the altar of the Temple to be erected on Mount Moriah in Jerusalem?

❧

Along with Aaron, his sons and the seventy Elders I ascended Sinai soon after the embers died upon the altars. God asked me to ascend further. I arose with Joshua, my loyal student, who would later wait at the mountainside the forty days until I returned. I asked the Elders to wait but leave responsibility for the Congregation in the hands of Aaron and Hur, my nephew, Miriam's son. (I would never again see Hur alive. He was killed forty days later trying to stave off the rebellion in the shadow of the Golden Calf.)

"And those men lifted me up from there, and they carried me up to the seventh heaven. And I saw there an exceptionally great light, and all the fiery armies of the archangels, and the incorporeal forces and the... cherubim and the seraphim and the many-eyed thrones....And then they went to their places in joy and merriment and in immeasurable light, singing songs with soft and gentle voices, while presenting the liturgy to Him gloriously." (2 Enoch [J] 20:1–4)

I labored halfway up the Mountain, walking into a thick cloud. The sunlight was blocked by the cloud, and day passed to night and back again, six times. Time, for me, stood still. I wept endlessly, uncertain whether my tears were of joy for what Sinai might represent in Eternity, or in torment for our sins.

As I strode into the furnace, I suffered badly. I feared that I might be offered up, as our forefather Isaac almost was—but, here, to appease God for the faithlessness that the Israelites had shown continually since the Exodus. I wondered if I myself would become a "sacrifice" for all time, executed atop the darkened Sinai. I feared that my blood would be an "absolution" for all the Congregation's sins—

those already committed and those still to be committed by the Israelites' descendants. And, finally, I trembled madly over whether if when it was nearly over and having concluded that He had forsaken me, I would need to beseech our Father to forgive them for having known not what they did.

As if in a trance, I began to accept and almost will a personal martyrdom that seemed to be in the offing. I feared, too, that my martyrdom as a sacrificial lamb might make me a "god" to a people that had become so reckless when facing despair.

But the six days passed quickly, and He called on me to ascend higher. I followed the Voice.

Twice in my life I would climb to near the top of Sinai. The first was six days after the Ten Pronouncements were imparted at the height of our hopefulness. It was a time when the Congregation's past sins seemed to have been erased, and my hopefulness was complete.

The second was after I descended Sinai, only to learn that my hopeful ascendancy had fallen into a valley of faithlessness never before known. It was when I would ascend again to obtain a second set of Tablets.

But I would spend the second forty days learning how to beg forgiveness from a God so

"Moses remained on the mountain for 40 days and 40 nights while the Lord showed him what [was] beforehand as well as what was to come. He related to him the divisions of all the times, both of the Torah and of the 'testimony.' He said to him:… 'Now you write this entire message which I am telling you today…then this testimony will serve as evidence.'"
(Jubilees 1:4–8)

quickly abandoned by His chosen people. It seems that the first ascent to learn the Torah would have been useless without the second. Simple "knowledge" that lacks ability to seek forgiveness yields knowledge for its own sake.

The first forty days were the most pristine days of my life. I rested against a barren mountainside that was bathed in a hue that made the Mountain different than at any other time. The Written Word never describes the forty days, except to say that I neither ate nor drank, and that on the last day before I descended I "argued" with God, to persuade Him to not destroy the Israelites.

I taught the people over the next forty years in the desert all of the Torah that I received during those forty days. But during those days atop the Mountain I would not learn the Written Word. Most of it has come during these last three weeks. The "Torah" that I learned atop Sinai was actually all of His laws and ordinances and their interpretations. They were not the narrative stories of the Written Torah, but a code of conduct.

Most of my days atop the Mountain I simply sat and listened to the Voice. It was perhaps a voice that would have been inaudible to anyone else who had mistakenly climbed the Mountain and had joined me. It was a voice, though, that would have been audible to me, even if I were deaf.

And although it seemed that the Voice frequently revealed God's annoyance with my limitations in understanding His Word, later I wondered if the displeasure actually came from within myself.

Much of what He told me was, indeed, too difficult to understand. My face surely disclosed what He saw, that is, my mind's limits. But when I tortured myself to understand Him and thus came to better understand His meaning, the experience was more satisfying. I was persuaded by His Voice that He, too, became more satisfied with me.

Still, did I become a better man for having obtained greater knowledge than the other Israelites? And would they who learned less than I, but exerted themselves more to acquire the knowledge, not have accomplished more? And is it not better still to use the knowledge to become a better person? Would a "better" person not be perceived by God as having climbed higher on Mount Sinai than me?

It was curious that the Written Torah describes my stay atop Sinai so tersely. Did He want those days and nights to remain shrouded in mystery? Did He want the Israelites to speculate on the mystery of the Oral Torah? Did God envision our descendants searching for nuance, refinement and distinction in interpreting His

"Then He [God] said to me [Ezra], 'I revealed myself in a bush and spoke to Moses, when my people were in bondage in Egypt; and I sent him and I led my people out of Egypt and I led him up to Mt. Sinai. And I kept him with me many days. And I told him many wondrous things, and showed him the secrets of the times and declared to him the end of the times. Then I commanded him, saying, 'These words you shall publish openly, and these you shall keep secret." (4 Ezra 14:3–6; also 14:37–47)

Law? Would a flat statement in the text describing, soberly, what had occurred atop Mount Sinai have undermined His true intention? And did He deliberately leave unexplained words and thoughts in the text, thus, to encourage concentration on its true meaning?

〜

Laws that require abstention from sins of the flesh are surely difficult to observe. It is not a burden much eased by logic. Still, the logic of such laws that consumed much of my stay at Sinai did ease their intake.

But whether by design or not, He daily entangled the process. Often, He instructed me on laws that find no basis in human understanding. The timing with which they arrived seemed almost playful on this part. Thus, these laws, not understandable but often pivotal to our daily life, were not always taught at sunrise, when my mind was freshest. Nor did they arrive at nightfall, when the day's instruction had matured my sense of Him, or even when the sun was highest in the sky.

"You shall keep my statutes. You shall not let your animals breed with a different kind…"
(Lev 19:19)

So the learning process yielded this added agony. I was forced to try to understand the new odd law that always seemed to arrive, strangely, just after a command so easily understood.

"…you shall not sow your field with two kinds of seed…"
(Lev 19:19)

How, after all, did He chose precisely when to teach me, for example, not to mate an animal into another species? Nor to plant a field with mixed seed? Nor to wear a garment of a mixture of wool and linen? For such ordinances all came instantly after He commanded that we "love our neighbor as ourself"—a rule of easy understanding. It was almost as if He wanted me to lapse into a spell of fear and fault myself for not understanding.

"...nor shall you put on a garment made of two different materials." (Lev 19:19)

I would perhaps have been spared this fear if I knew that although a new mystery might arrive each day, it would do so only at dawn, or dusk, or midnight. I could thereby plan to await the clandestine and recognize its arrival, not be frustrated by a mystery that might not be understood in mankind's terms.

The timing, however, would never allay my worst nightmare: Upon my descent to teach the Congregation what I had learned, but could not explain, they would find me to be a fraud who had created his own mysteries only to deify himself.

So, as I awaited the hidden tenet, I agonized to find sense and meaning for every law He gave me. Curiously, He never impeded such a pursuit, and perhaps encouraged that I do so. That is, until, or that is at least until I thought, I had found it.

"...[Y]ou shall love your neighbor as yourself: I am the LORD." (Lev 19:18)

But, in an instantaneous spell of *kabbalism* I found meaning for every law He gave. I knew, *really knew,* why the Israelites could not eat of animals that lack split hoofs and do not chew their cud. I *knew,* at that moment, why crustaceans could not be eaten. I decrypted the mystery that proscribed garments woven of linen and wool. No longer was there for me any secret in the Red Heifer.

And, finally, I was no longer mystified by the ultimate mystery: Why had He left to the seemingly "occult" these many personal sacrifices He thus dictated? I, thus, found true meaning and reason for *every* law that for so long had seemed to defy reason.

But, finally, at that wondrous moment, when it seemed that I had pierced the secret meaning of too much, when I had come perilously close to trespassing the state of God, my world seemed to burst. The dream in which all the answers had come to me was now ended, and I was disconnected from His true meaning as before: the danger in reaching too close to the flame.

It was not that during the forty days atop Sinai, or in the forty years to follow, I was unwilling to question, or even challenge, His Ways. I actively sought to conscript logic or even human emotion, all to make sense of Him.

"He said, 'Take your son, your only son Isaac, whom you love, and go to the land of Moriah, and offer him there as a burnt offering on one of the mountains that I shall show you.'"
(Gen 22:2)

As but one example of the talmudic encounter at Sinai—I would posit that God had not been satisfied in simply testing Abraham as He did at Moriah. I imagined that God had carried through in demanding that Abraham actually let his hatchet fall across Isaac's throat, as proof of his love of God. I myself would have been horrified even by the thought of it. And I would have been dismayed if, at Sinai, He commanded the Congregation to resign itself to a practice of human sacrifice.

My love of God notwithstanding, I, Moses, though never pressed to it, would not have passed the test of Abraham. If God had asked me to kill my children, I would never have heard the Voice at the Burning Bush, or ever after.

I am troubled that if the generations knew this they might alter their belief in God, given such flaws in my own commitment. My flaws, indeed, are increased by a fear that I secretly question God for having pushed Abraham even to that point He did. And my flaws continue in believing that animal sacrifice was merely God's ploy to wean the Congregation from a world of other nations who condoned human sacrifice.

But in my pondering the story of Abraham, I am reminded that the Congregation must not eat pig for reasons I cannot comprehend. And unlike human sacrifice, this law I *will* indeed follow to the death, and urge the Congregation to follow.

And death may follow. For he instructed me that if I refuse to eat pig, my vengeful enemy may demand that I bow to his god at penalty of death. God tells me that I must die, rather than bow to idols. Do I not thus take my own life and, so, engage in human sacrifice? And though I have drawn my own line at human sacrifice, would I not also tell my son to fall on the same sword, rather than bow to an idol. Have I drawn a line in shifting sand?

To deal with all of this, does the Torah simply allow me to tell my son that there are things worth dying for? And, if so, why did Abraham, the model of the faithful, not tell Isaac, when the moment of truth was at hand for both, that death may be the most compelling moment in a righteous man's life?

❧

This give and take, this attempt to conquer the sometimes incomprehensible, was what learning the Torah was like at Sinai.

And I wondered whether to accomplish what I did upon the Mountain, does anyone need to hear a Supreme Being speak to him atop a mountain? And, finally, was this intricate form of learning designed to eliminate the temptations of the world that we yielded to so easily at the foot of the Mountain?

Chapter 10
The Golden Calf

When the people saw that Moses delayed to come down from the mountain, the people gathered around Aaron, and said to him, "Come, make gods for us, who shall go before us; as for this Moses, the man who brought us up out of the land of Egypt, we do not know what has become of him." Aaron said to them, "Take off the gold rings that are on the ears of your wives, your sons, and your daughters, and bring them to me." So all the people took off the gold rings from their ears, and brought them to Aaron. He took the gold from them, formed it in a mold, and cast an image of a calf; and they said, "These are your gods, O Israel, who brought you up out of the land of Egypt!" When Aaron saw this, he built an altar before it; and Aaron made proclamation and said, "Tomorrow shall be a festival to the LORD."

> They rose early the next day, and offered burnt
> offerings and brought sacrifices of well-being;
> and the people sat down to eat and drink, and
> rose up to revel.
>
> The LORD said to Moses, "Go down at
> once! Your people, whom you brought up out of
> the land of Egypt, have acted perversely; they
> have been quick to turn aside from the way that
> I commanded them; they have cast for them-
> selves an image of a calf, and have worshiped it
> and sacrificed to it, and said, 'These are your
> gods, O Israel, who brought you up out of the
> land of Egypt!'" The LORD said to Moses, "I have
> seen this people, how stiff-necked they are. Now
> let me alone, so that my wrath may burn hot
> against them and I may consume them; and of
> you I will make a great nation."
>
> (Exod 32:1–10)

Aside from the words He Himself has authored, there are
no truths—only versions.

I rest against this rock to recall events I once experienced,
thoughts I used to think and observations I arrive at now. These
silent thoughts are for myself, here and now—a brief escape on
this last day of my journey. They exist not for always, for the generations will never know them. They are personal thoughts of an
old man. Hard as I try, though, to make my mind capture things
as they truly were, I fail.

A people's past, a person's life is shaded, influenced by whether the author is a victor, or someone vanquished. They depend on whether the protagonists were brusque or gentle; whether one tells his story walking up a hill, or down; whether a pleasing aroma blows in the breeze, or a baby's laughter eases the painful account of man's war; whether one's death is imminent at his narration; or, whether time's passage or a forgiveness bestowed has softened the harshness of events, and made mellow the torments once imposed.

He never asked me at Sinai to write His Story. Were that task mine, my stay atop the Mountain would have lasted longer. My accounts would have been more expansive; my judgments of others less stinging, more vague. My narrations would have been more lenient to those who warrant a pedestal, in memory.

This is not in tribute to my capacity for compassion. Rather, it would be for fear that the mountain we must climb might be too steep for the weak, or those of weakened spirit; for fear that they might fall by the wayside or abandon the climb, frustrated by its torturing slope.

Those of tomorrow may fear this too, and wish to flatten the road as do I now in private meditation on things past.

To make the journey easier for the needy of spirit, to bring them more safely to their destiny is a noble goal that surely merits His praise. It may even be God's will that we enlarge the deserving in death beyond what they were in life, lest those who follow long hereafter be confused by the faults of their heroes who come before.

But if we outright strip away our heroes' flaws, we may rush to places where angels should not go. If we violate plain meaning to make right their wrongs, if we interpret their conduct to make them gods, not men of weakness, we risk repeating the sin of the Golden Calf committed in the shadow of Sinai.

"Now let me alone, so that my wrath may burn hot against them and I may consume them; and of you I will make a great nation." But Moses implored the LORD his God, and said, "O LORD, why does your wrath burn hot against your people, whom you brought out of the land of Egypt with great power and with a mighty hand? Why should the Egyptians say, 'It was with evil intent that he brought them out to kill them in the mountains…'"
(Exod 32:10–12)

My descent from Sinai began, my heart in my mouth. My blood coursed through me. It raced like a runaway animal wounded during an encounter with danger, knowing that further danger lurked ahead.

I full knew the grief that awaited me at the foot of the Mountain; but strangely, I was relieved as the descent began. I was relieved that God had relented on His plan to annihilate the Israelites for contriving the Calf.

Still, I never really nurtured a belief that He would fulfill his threat. The Written Word says that my plea to God—that the Egyptians would mock Him for liberating the Israelites, only to kill them and breach His promise to Abraham—persuaded Him. My belief persists, though, that while His anger was great, His words were only exaggeration.

I supposed my son having lost trust in me, for having been absent too long, and my servant, my companion in raising him, had likewise been missing to him. What if my son left my home and took a new father, a flawed replacement chosen by him only to demonstrate his disgust in having lost me? And in the process, I supposed, my son mocked me.

I would be thunderstruck—hurt beyond repair, driven to unending tears, scandalized among my friends and family. I might even, in utter pain be moved to say the words: "I will kill him." But might any decent man, faced even with such rejection, kill the very son he nurtured?

Am I not a child of God, created in His image? Is His capacity to forgive not greater than mine? Would God have killed those he nurtured and redeemed from slavery, even facing a betrayal so offensive to His Commandments as the Calf? No. My arguments did not save His people from God's wrath. It was His quality of forgiveness.

But in deciding how God might have acted, do I do not take liberty with the limits of man's vision—trying to reckon how He would act, by how we would? Should we presume to gauge God's ways by the responses that we as His children would give?

The path downward was steep, and I walked slowly. My further delay no longer mattered. The damage was done already. The people would later say, to excuse themselves, that they had mistaken the date of my return by a single day. And for that alone, they openly violated the Commandments He gave just weeks before. What added misfortune could my slow pace bring—even if I were to dawdle and thus delay seeing for myself the horrendous spectacle ahead? Would rushing to see their treachery lessen in my own mind my failures as a leader? Could I worsen the truth that just one day's mistake could enable them to contrive a Golden Calf to replace God?

Surely, my reason for delaying would be criticized, if known. Since the Burning Bush, I was responsible for all the people: all those who related back to Abraham, or chose to enter his covenant with God. No longer was I only responsible for the bloodlines of my father and mother alone.

In this crisis, though, when the people had failed Him so, my only worry was the "blood of *my* blood." First among them was my brother Aaron. He was my fellow in all that was Divine for us: God's true warrior when I lacked faith to battle Pharaoh. He was the High Priest, the tower among men, alone fit to repent Israel's sins. He was the only man trusted to guide them, when I ascended to receive the Torah.

I agonized, finding reasons to rest along my descent—imagining what had happened to Aaron. Had they killed him in an eruptive loss of faith, when he decried their sinful ways? Did they torture him and threaten death for his family, making him incapable of restraint? Had he taken his own life? Did he die the sufferer's death in God's name, rather than aid the worship of an idol? Did he himself lose faith—had the slavery in Egypt taken its toll on him, too?

What bothered me most as I neared the ground was deciding which, in my *own* eyes, was worse. Would I rather see my brother, who yielded to the mob and participated in their mortal sin, alive? Or would I rather see him dead for having reproached its idolatry?

God, of course, already knew what had happened. My difficulty was not what it might mean to God, but what it meant to me. That, more than anything, disgraced me in my own eyes. To be committed to God, did I need to hope to see my brother dead?

My agony ended when I reached the savannah adjacent the mountain. I saw a blur of lewdness encircling the Calf. The warnings God gave me hours earlier at the mountain peak could never prepare me for this, or restrain my arms as they took control of my body.

Seemingly only in an instant, I threw the Tablets to the ground; I then proceeded to melt the Calf. I sprinkled its dust into a potion to be fed to the assembled sinners. The Torah describes these acts of rage, but I cannot recall them. My mind was elsewhere and my acts were uncontrolled as the confrontation awaited me.

Aaron sat on the ground as I labored to approach him. My eyes were so focused on him that the thousands of sinners drinking their idol's dust were invisible to me. Aaron looked like a wounded sheep as he sat near the broken pedestal where the Calf had been perched. He seemed to have aged thirty years since I saw him last just a few weeks before.

"As soon as he came near the camp and saw the calf and the dancing, Moses' anger burned hot, and he threw the tablets from his hands and broke them at the foot of the mountain. He took the calf that they had made, burned it with fire, ground it to powder, scattered it on the water, and made the Israelites drink it." (Exod 32:19–20)

I searched his head and arms for scars or signs of blood-stain. My eyes refused to meet his. His sheepish manner as I approached did not allow me to show respect even to my own brother.

I asked him, *"What did this people do to you that you have brought so great a sin upon them?"* (Exod 32:21). He answered slowly, while tears dropped down his face. I began to ask him again when, with a quivering voice, he started to answer. As he began to speak, he tried to touch my arm. It was a brotherly ges-ture to help allay his own embarrassment, or mine. I pushed his arm aside, as if he were a wayward child whose conduct demanded my rebuke. I will never forgive myself for that act.

And Aaron said, *"Do not let the anger of my lord burn hot; you know the people, that they are bent on evil. They said to me, 'Make us gods, who shall go before us; as for this Moses, the man who brought us up out of the land of Egypt, we do not know what has become of him.' So I said to them, 'Whoever has gold, take it off'; so they gave it to me, and I threw it into the fire, and out came this calf!"* (Exod 32:22–24)

When his words ended, I inwardly wished that Aaron had killed himself, or had been murdered in defending God's Law. Faith sometimes asks too much.

But to the end of his account, Aaron was a man of integrity. He was correct—"This people was disposed toward evil." I began to think that an excuse would lie at the end of his response. But he offered none. More important, he offered none for himself. He would not mitigate, not condone, nor excuse. He offered no words to make his actions in response to the mob a pretense to stretch time until I descended from Sinai. Nor, curiously, were there words of apology.

Some will surely say that Aaron could only have been God's later choice to be High Priest if he had good reason for his actions. They will say that he had, indeed, engaged in a scheming stall for time, and did not become an aider in the ultimate act of idolatory. For surely a sinner of the dimension depicted in black and white could not have been fit to repent his own sins, let alone those of us all as High Priest.

But He offered no such words. Perhaps because for a man to whom integrity was paramount, no false excuse would be used to lessen his wrong. So he surfaced none, despite my anger that begged for words of defense or explanation.

Whatever Aaron's reason, looking for an excuse for Aaron's (or others') transgressions, is not a judgment that mortals should make. Aaron was my brother. His blessed memory will live with me forever. Aaron stood tall when I failed God at the Burning Bush. And when he died, the people mourned him so. They had lost a cloud of protection, a shield that hovered above us along the wandering journey. When he died the people were no longer shielded from the blistering sun, the cold desolation of the desert night, the feared onslaught of our enemies and the gripping vise of inner torment and indecision. Aaron was truly a priest—*the*

Priest among all our people. His name will shine on the entablatures of decency and honesty forever.

But, still, Aaron did fail *that day*. God's text does not permit an alternative to the blackness of black or whiteness of white.

Despite all, God, in his ineffable wisdom, chose to forgive Aaron. We should not give tortured reasons for why God would forgive men like Aaron, whose conduct, that *one day*, seems to have been so wrong.

For us to "flatten the road" by presuming that Aaron did no wrong in order thus to "explain" God's thinking in the reckoning He accords in reward and punishment for man's acts, deifies ourselves and is wrong. It is a wrong that confounds us with God, and confuses the judgments we would make if we were Him, with those He alone must make.

It denies God's willingness to forgive our sins, no matter how grievous—as He did that very day at Sinai when, first, He threatened our annihilation.

Chapter 11
Slaughter at Sinai

When Moses saw that the people were running wild (for Aaron had let them run wild, to the derision of their enemies), then Moses stood in the gate of the camp, and said, "Who is on the LORD's side? Come to me!" And all the sons of Levi gathered around him. He said to them, "Thus says the LORD, the God of Israel, 'Put your sword on your side, each of you! Go back and forth from gate to gate throughout the camp, and each of you kill your brother, your friend, and your neighbor.'" The sons of Levi did as Moses commanded, and about three thousand of the people fell on that day. Moses said, "Today you have ordained yourselves for the service of the LORD, each one at the cost of a son or a brother, and so have brought a blessing on yourselves this day."

(Exod 32:25–29)

"...Moses now
gathered new
courage to
intercede for
Israel. He said:
'O Lord of the
world! Israel has
indeed created a
rival for Thee in
their idol, that
Thou are angry
with them. The
calf, I supposed,
shall bid stars
and moon to
appear, while
Thou makest the
sun to rise; Thou
shalt send the
dew and he will
cause the wind to
blow; Thou shalt
send down the
rain, and he shall
bid the plants
to grow.' God:
'Moses, thou
are mistaken,
like them, and
knowest not that
the idol is
absolutely
nothing...'"
(ShR 42–4; Tan
Ki-Tissa 21–24;
Legends III)

As I laid down to rest each night during the seven weeks beginning the night of Exodus, I inwardly came, despite all, to relish my role. Despite all the second thoughts, all the murmurs, I was His choice to lead the glorious redemption of a people.

But the people never participated in that choice as they labored in the slave camps at Pithom and Rameses; or the night we left Egypt; or at the shores of the Red Sea; or during the disheartening struggles along the desert journey; or even at the foot of Sinai; or ever.

And, unlike in the instance of the anointment of Pharaoh, the only other leader they ever knew, my selection was not born in a tradition that spanned the preceding generations. No precedent gave them hopefulness to believe that the torch of leadership *truly* belonged in my hand. Nor could they be satisfied that their fathers or grandfathers would have accepted the process that trumpeted it. For despite His pronouncement at the Burning Bush, the "leader" of the congregation was imposed on them by a Force whose throne was never seen by them. And their constant murmurings were proof enough of their dissatisfaction—my "anointment" notwithstanding.

Descending from Sinai, the glee that I experienced nightly for seven weeks and during the happy forty days on the Mountain, quickly ended. The people descended into lewdness at the foot of Sinai—a lawless people had repudiated His commands. I saw not simply an open loss of faith in the Almighty. Instead, what confronted me as their leader was a rebellion. It was not only an insurrection against God; more directly for me, it was an insurrection against the rule of law and their "anointed" leader whom He had just threatened with the nation's destruction. Those calamitous words were frightening, when I first perceived the extent of their anarchy.

This, then, was the exquisite moment to decide that I must lead them. I could not abdicate, even if He would let me, nor allow them to reject me in favor of a leader of their own choice. I feared that if that new leader would reject His Commandments in favor of the pagan ways I saw that day, the impending fate of the Canaanites would engulf the Israelites, too. I needed to be a "leader" to protect them from themselves. Sometimes, it came to me, that that is the meaning of leadership. To not firmly seize the reins, but simply remain God's speaker, was now unthinkable.

But leadership, indeed one needed to quell an insurrection, sometimes requires the unthinkable.

❧

God pronounced a death sentence for those who choose to worship idols. No one can doubt the clarity of His decree. But God never ordered me that day, when He told me of the Golden Calf, to decree that *"every man kill his brother"*—as I declared in His name. The direction was my own; my first exercise of true leadership. The Levites killed no one. I, myself, killed the three thousand. If taking one's own life, though, were not against His edicts, I, too, would have fallen that day.

Surely, leaders in the generations to follow will suffer pangs of guiltiness, even if confident in the wisdom of their decisions. For occasionally death, even the deaths of one's own people, is preferable to the consequences of the alternative. That is the price of a war among one's own people—even a *Holy* such war.

My choice was justified. I know that now. Still, that night I heard again the words I heard many years before when I fled Egypt: *"Who appointed you as a dignitary, a ruler and a judge over us?"* I wondered if Pharaoh felt as I did that night, on that terrible day for him when, at his demand, his men risked death in the Sea of Reeds. We share a common bind; we both ordered the killing of our own men in the name of personal belief, and both survived to report their deaths.

History, though, is written by the victors. It will tell the generations to follow that I acted nobly that day. Yet the account of my "victory" over the rebellion will omit the nightly tears I shed over how I chose to "save" my people.

Chapter 12
The Mask

Moses came down from Mount Sinai. As he came down from the mountain with the two tablets of the covenant in his hand, Moses did not know that the skin of his face shone because he had been talking with God. When Aaron and all the Israelites saw Moses, the skin of his face was shining, and they were afraid to come near him.
(Exod 34:29–30)

When Moses had finished speaking with them, he put a veil on his face; but whenever Moses went in before the LORD to speak with him, he would take the veil off, until he came out; and when he came out, and told the Israelites what he had been commanded, the Israelites would see the face of Moses, that the skin of his face was

*shining; and Moses would put the veil on his face
again, until he went in to speak with him.* (Exod
34:33–35)

Each of us hides behind a mask.

We shield our face from the penetrating rays of the noon-day sun. We deny our enemy knowledge that the encounter with them grips us. We persuade our family that we lack fear of the unknown, when fright, indeed, consumes us. We hide indiffer-ence to the plight of our neighbor, when we are selfishly con-cerned with ourselves.

This is the mask of mankind: a superficial outer gesture; a device to hide the truth and reality beneath.

A dread overcame the people when I had descended from Sinai, for my exposed face reminded them that sinning at the Golden Calf denied them the opportunity for God's glow to envelop them. My mask would protect them from that harsh and painful reminder.

The rudimentary mask, though, would become an off-putting uniform to ironically remind them of their sin, and thereby insulate me from the people. No longer could I walk without being recognized, even on the borders of the camp where the people would not otherwise recognize me as His supposed exemplar.

But most of all, my mask would be unlike the mask worn by others. It was, of course, designed to protect the *people* from what my face would say to them about *themselves*. But this mask would also secretly protect me from what my face would say about *me*. The reality was that my life, too, was flawed and overcome by fear: the fear of paralysis, of all-consuming fright and indifference to my fellow man. Strangely, then, my mask uniquely protected both *them* and *me*.

Or did the mask become something else? Did it become an ironic reminder to all that the more we paint a false face on reality, the more the attempt at deception discloses what lies within?

Chapter 13
Miriam

...Miriam and Aaron spoke against Moses because of the Cushite woman whom he had married (for he had indeed married a Cushite woman); and they said, "Has the LORD spoken only through Moses? Has he not spoken through us also?" And the LORD heard it. Now the man Moses was very humble, more so than anyone else on the face of the earth. Suddenly the LORD said to Moses, Aaron, and Miriam, "Come out, you three, to the tent of meeting." So the three of them came out. Then the LORD came down in a pillar of cloud, and stood at the entrance of the tent, and called Aaron and Miriam; and they both came forward. And he said, "Hear my words: When there are prophets among you, I the LORD make myself known to them in visions; I speak to them in dreams. Not so with my servant Moses; he is entrusted with all my house.

With him I speak face to face—clearly, not in riddles; and he beholds the form of the LORD….
(Num 12:1–8)

"…Why then were you not afraid to speak against my servant Moses?" And the anger of the LORD was kindled against them, and he departed.
(Num 12:8–9)

When the cloud went away from over the tent, Miriam had become leprous, as white as snow….Then Aaron said to Moses, "Oh, my lord, do not punish us for a sin that we have so foolishly committed….And Moses cried to the LORD, "O God, please heal her." But the LORD said to Moses, "If her father had but spit in her face, would she not bear her shame for seven days? Let her be shut out of the camp for seven days, and after that she may be brought in again…."
(Num 12:10–16)

My sister Miriam came before me. Without her, I would never have been.

My mother told me, when I was first old enough to understand, that my Miriam was also a mother to me. Faced with

Pharaoh's "War Against the Male Hebrew Baby," my father Amram withdrew from my mother, fearing that a male born of them would be born only to die. Miriam, still a child herself, but a seer, persuaded him in secret that his own act of surrender was worse than Pharaoh's own decree. For it prevented the birth of baby girls, and possibly even a "Redeemer." Our father relented under Miriam's exquisite act of private admonition.

Private admonition: the purest means of useful persuasion.

Miriam's role in my escaping Pharaoh's edict of infant killing did not end there. At three months, at our mother's urging, Miriam placed me in a basket in the bulrushes along the river's edge. She protected me at my most vulnerable. I was, then, a "prophet" incapable of caring for myself; perceiving basic danger; or dealing with the harsh effects of the Egyptian sun. I was a defenseless, naked baby—and Miriam knew all the flaws in her infant sibling's armor, as only an older sibling would. She would continue to.

For Miriam, I was in some ways always a plaything. No matter God's Plan, she would always recall that when I was naked and exposed in that basket, Miriam was the superior figure—my protector. Nothing would change that truth in our relationship.

As Miriam would still me when she feared that I might cry and compromise my safety along the river's edge, so, too, in her sisterly way, she believed that she could still me for a lifetime, when my actions might undermine a oneness with her views.

As my motherly sister, she surely believed—as I never discouraged it—that given her roles in my birth and nursing, my conduct would always conform to her opinions. To her, it wouldn't matter how far from the basket I traveled, the relationships I would enter along my life's journey, or my needs that would become my destiny. One's bond with a sibling in his early years becomes more pronounced along their passing years. Having saved my life, in some mystical way I actually owed my life to her.

Miriam, though, was not the only woman to save my life. Years later, when God became enraged and sought to kill me, Zipporah, in an uncommon act of valor, circumcised her own son to save my life. But I never felt that her personal sacrifice would oblige my having to submit to her perception of what road my life should take.

Was it a disparity in the two women who, each, had saved my life? Was it that Miriam was my protector when I was totally exposed—as only an elder sibling would have been? Or is it that only the spell of an older sibling or parent will enforce the "duty"? Strangely, though, my relationship with Zipporah later would become the reason why God punished Miriam.

"On the way, at a place where they spent the night, the LORD met him [Moses] and tried to kill him. But Zipporah took a flint and cut off her son's foreskin, and touched Moses' feet with it, and said, 'Truly you are a bridegroom of blood to me!' So he let him alone. It was then she said, 'A bridegroom of blood by circumcision.'" (Exod 4:24–26)

What was it that caused Miriam to speak ill of me—even though Miriam, Aaron and I were all grown and each had marched along God's path?

Some say that Miriam was annoyed that I had withdrawn from relations from Zipporah. To them, she felt that I had pretentiously concluded that I alone needed constant purity to pursue God's dictates, and therefore withdrew from the uncleanliness of the physical.

Some leaders, sinfully, yield to temptations of the flesh or greed or hero-worship. My great regret is that somehow my sin was worse. Like my father before Miriam admonished him, I, too, "withdrew" from my family, but for another reason.

It was not for the compelling reason that moved my father. Nor was it because of my supposed purity—that I needed to be purer than my siblings to do God's work. Instead it was because of a passion for my "duty" to my flock—a flock frequently without water, or food, or faith. I became so rapt by "duty," that I ignored the duty of intimacy with those to whom I was unalterably attached and obligated. I ignored those few individuals to whom promises must be kept, despite what God imposed on me as his "anointed of the Congregation."

Leaders who allow their duties to family to be alienated, thus, by a duty to strangers no matter how beloved, betray their true role as exemplars. I did, and Miriam, my elder sister, recognized it. And surely it appalled her.

But my many faults aside, I was not distant from Miriam. Miriam would not have hesitated to confront me with such a withdrawal, no matter what it was.

No. Her disillusion with me lay elsewhere. She was not bothered by what I had done in my marriage, but to whom I was married. Not Zipporah herself, whom Miriam admired greatly—but what she represented. In the Bible's words: *"...Miriam and Aaron spoke against Moses because of the Cushite woman whom he had married (for he had indeed married a Cushite woman)."*

Years earlier, despairing in my exile, my need for the love of a woman let me "stray" from our people—even though the woman I loved, Zipporah, was covenantally committed to God.

Miriam's unhappiness was that Zipporah not only was not in the daughterhood of our Matriarch Sarah, but also was an Ethiopian whose dark skin was a constant reminder of that fact that would never change. For Miriam, I was God's exemplar who chose to propagate with a dark-skinned gentile—even one who so believed in God. This issue Miriam could not bring to me to discuss. For like Zipporah's ancestry, Miriam knew that my love for Zipporah would also never change.

God Himself never questioned my choice of a wife, whose belief in God became my constant

"...Moses had determined, as soon as his sister became diseased, to intercede for her with God, saying to himself: 'It is not right that my sister should suffer and I dwell in contentment.' He now drew a circle about himself, stood up, and said a short prayer to God, which he closed with the words: 'I will not go from this spot until Thou shalt have healed my sister. But if Thou do not heal her, I myself shall do so, for Thou hast already revealed to me, how leprosy arises and how it disappears...'"
(Sifre N, 106; Legends III)

inspiration. Just as He never questioned the decision by Joseph, indeed, "Joseph the Righteous," son of our forefather Jacob, to marry a woman gentile at birth. The reason is simple: My choice did not offend the "God" of the Israelites—only their culture. Or, in the murmurings in the camp: "Were our sisters not good enough for you?"

Surely, we must be exhaustibly cautious, lest our sons and daughters stray from our people's bloodline—but not through a bias that uses His name to warrant exclusion or rejection. What would it say about us if, in the ages to follow, Cushites, who suffered so to believe in, were excluded from acceptance in the Promised Land?

Miriam was a prophetess, truly a Woman of Valor. I prayed fervently for her recovery, and wished so badly that He had not, thus, punished her. She herself taught in her youth the lesson that private admonition and discussion were the keys to open doors to reconciliation. But it was a lesson that eluded her when it came to this troubling issue.

The sad irony is that the penalty for Miriam's chastising me over the blackness of Zipporah was the whiteness of the affliction that condemned her.

Chapter 14
The Spies

The LORD said to Moses, "Send men to spy out the land of Canaan, which I am giving to the Israelites; from each of their ancestral tribes you shall send a man, every one a leader among them." (Num 13:1–2)

Moses sent them to spy out the land of Canaan, and said to them, "Go up there into the Negeb, and go up into the hill country, and see what the land is like, and whether the people who live in it are strong or weak, whether they are few or many, and whether the land they live in is good or bad, and whether the towns that they live in are unwalled or fortified...." (Num 13:17–19)

89

So they went up and spied out the land....At the end of forty days they returned from spying out the land....And they told him, "Yet the people who live in the land are strong, and the towns are fortified and very large; and besides, we saw the descendants of Anak there. The Amalekites live in the land of the Negeb....There we saw the Nephilim (the Anakites come from the Nephilim); and to ourselves we seemed like grasshoppers, and so we seemed to them."

(Num 13:2, 25, 27–29, 33)

Then all the congregation raised a loud cry, and the people wept that night. And all the Israelites complained against Moses and Aaron; the whole congregation said to them, "Would that we had died in the land of Egypt! Or would that we had died in this wilderness!...So they said to one another, "Let us choose a captain, and go back to Egypt." (Num 14:1–2, 4)

And the LORD spoke to Moses and to Aaron, saying: How long shall this wicked congregation complain against me?...Say to them, "As I live," says the LORD, "I will do to you the very things I heard you say: your dead bodies shall fall in

*this very wilderness; and of all your number,
included in the census, from twenty years old
and upward, who have complained against
me....But as for you, your dead bodies shall fall
in this wilderness. And your children shall be
shepherds in the wilderness for forty years, and
shall suffer for your faithlessness, until the last of
your dead bodies lies in the wilderness."*

(Num 14:26–29, 32–33)

I held my hand in salute against my forehead, to shield my eyes from the sun—anticipating, with all the rest, the arrival of twelve Princes of Israel. We expected men who had tasted the "milk and honey," men who would predict imminent victory to regain the Promised Land. But as they approached the camp, even near the horizon, I would shield my eyes no longer. I preferred the blinding sun to the doom foretold by the halting carriage of these humbled men.

As they came into view they seemed like crippled hunchbacks, more stooped over with every lumbering step as they edged toward the camp. Only two, Joshua and Caleb, Miriam's husband, stood erect, separating themselves from the rest. Despite their confident bearing, they looked over their shoulders, shamed by the despair of those who dragged behind. They later tore their garments in mourning over the seeming death of their brothers inflicted by their own defeated spirit.

As the Princes came closer, they were like wounded warriors returning from defeat, though no enemy had engaged

"And Joshua son of Nun and Caleb son of Jephunneh, who were among those who had spied out the land, tore their clothes and said to all the congregation... 'The land that we went through as spies is an exceedingly good land. If the LORD is pleased with us, he will bring us into this land and give it to us, a land that flows with milk and honey.... the LORD is with us; do not fear them.'"
(Num 14:6–9)

them. Their eyes could not meet the eyes of their families. They trembled as they moved, and stammered as they tried to speak. Sweat encompassed their bodies and the camp became sickened by their stench. They were humiliated, and humiliating to their listeners. Amalek, their brutal enemy of before, had doomed them again—this time without a sword. They were no longer princes, but miserable wretches lacking confidence in themselves. For them, God's signs and miracles were mirages from their past.

Nonetheless, should they have lied? Should they have told the throng that all was well—that the Nephilim, the prehistoric giants from the past, and the savage Amalekites did not rule the Land? Should they have deceived their people about their true perceptions—even if what they perceived was worse than what they observed?

Hard as I try, though, having never seen the Land *they* saw, I find no answer why death was needed to punish the spies for their hopefulness, even when it so demoralized a people. My thoughts are brief and unilluminating. They tell me simply that men and women may not always comprehend His wisdom. God, indeed, remains the Judge of Truth, even when uncomprehensibly a suckling baby dies: He alone knows the reasons.

And was it virtuous for God to condemn all the Congregation to live out their lives in the Wilderness for accepting the report that the Land appeared to be unconquerable? Should they have ignored the news that the danger they left behind at the shores of the Sea of Reeds awaited them again at the foothills of Canaan? Their princes, after all, until then, were men of uncommon valor.

There was, however, no unfairness. In reacting as they did to the spies' report they failed this ultimate test—a test perhaps not passable by a people who suffered from childhood in the pits of slavery. Their slavery, a prophecy to the future in their past, doomed both the spies and their tribes. They would always lack confidence not only in God, but also in themselves.

The listeners' reception to the spies' report told God what He himself needed to hear, and we needed to learn: Slavery does not end at liberation. It ends only when the slave, even a former slave, dies. To allow a generation of slaves, even those already unshackled, to enter, even conquer, Canaan would leave the conquest vulnerable from its beginning. Those to conquer the Land had to be the children, a people undaunted by the parents' hopelessness, imposed by a lifetime in shackles. Their children would reach the Land, and comforted by that knowledge the parents' remaining lives in the Wilderness would remain worthwhile.

God's decision to condemn the "liberated" slaves to live life out in the Wilderness was not pleasant for them to learn—but simply the way life, sometimes, has to be. I see that more clearly this moment of my life, as the air grows thinner with my every passing breath.

Chapter 15
Korah

*Now Korah son of Izhar son of Kohath son of
Levi, along with Dathan and Abiram...took two
hundred fifty Israelite men, leaders of the congregation, chosen from the assembly, well-
known men, and they confronted Moses. They
assembled against Moses and against Aaron, and
said to them, "You have gone too far! All the congregation are holy, every one of them, and the
LORD is among them. So why then do you exalt
yourselves above the assembly of the LORD?"
When Moses heard it, he fell on his face. Then he
said to Korah and all his company, "In the morning the LORD will make known who is his, and
who is holy, and who will be allowed to
approach him; the one whom he will choose he
will allow to approach him....." Then Moses said
to Korah, "Hear now, you Levites! Is it too little
for you that the God of Israel has separated you*

from the congregation of Israel, to allow you to approach him in order to perform the duties of the LORD's tabernacle, and to stand before the congregation and serve them...yet you seek the priesthood as well! Therefore you and all your company have gathered together against the LORD...." (Num 16:1–11)

Then the LORD spoke to Moses and to Aaron, saying: Separate yourselves from this congregation, so that I may consume them in a moment. They fell on their faces, and said, "O God, the God of the spirits of all flesh, shall one person sin and you become angry with the whole congregation?" (Num 16:20–22)

And Moses said, "This is how you shall know that the LORD has sent me to do all these works; it has not been of my own accord....But if the LORD creates something new, and the ground opens its mouth and swallows them up...then you shall know that these men have despised the LORD." (Num 16:28, 30)

> *The earth opened its mouth and swallowed them*
> *up, along with their households—everyone who*
> *belonged to Korah....*   (Num 16:32)

To some, the story of Korah will be the story of a rebel—a man who reached for power, but when he could not grasp it he became, at last, a bitter, petty divisive warrior; a man whose weapon words presented the illogical with logic, the impermissible with permissibility; a man whose oratory captivated both the lofty and the misbegotten with *seeming* persuasiveness. His gift would be to substitute truthfulness with the credible: credibility in place of honesty. He may seem in time to be a man for whom God's intercession, nothing less, was needed to cause his downfall.

But the story of Korah is not a story about Korah. It is about me.

In our youth, many believed that they saw through Korah's veneer of genius. To them, the motivating force in his quarrelsome manner was simply a goal to detract. But I, to whom words come slowly, with hardship, would secretly come to admire Korah.

It was lost on me that, though I walked in my youth in princely robe, the serpent-like manner of Korah's speech told all that he, not I, was reared for the purple. Korah would not need words to tell all that the exiled "prince" of Egypt, the would-be

Redeemer, was of heavy tongue. For the tongue of the serpent itself easily points, without words, to the creature he means to attack.

As I walked through the slave cities escorted by Egyptian guards, the due of a "prince," Korah would cease his insults against me in midsentence, lest my guards retaliate against him. He should well have known that he was safe from the scepter of Pharaoh that I carried; he knew that my understanding of his indignities, communicated in the language of the Hebrews, would go unpunished. My indefensible status as an "Egyptian" or perhaps my inability to rebut the skilled orator—would lead me to yield only gracious nods in retort. Korah surely believed that the shame of my dual origin would be my eventual undoing.

Once a guard believed he had heard Korah utter a personal insult against me that reflected also on Pharaoh. I made light of the remark and persuaded the guard that he misunderstood it. I couldn't then know that years later, I would be the one to encourage Korah's death warrant.

Korah would remain a minor irritant to me—a thorn in my side. I stayed my distance, although, time and again, the parry and thrust of his words bordered on attack on both me and my family. My irritation, though, would be controlled—for despite the double meaning in his every parry, he presented a stance of "respect" for God's Law. His disrespectful words were reserved for Aaron and me who presumed to speak for God. But always the crowd enjoyed the battles he conducted against we who presumed to joust with the illogic of his logically presented words.

❦

Life took us in different directions, and years passed before we would speak again.

I was now the Israelite "leader," and my brother Aaron was the High Priest. Now, Korah's envy was that of a man who was on the outside looking in—his nose pressed up against the outer curtain of the Holy of Holies. He was a strident believer in himself, now condemned to suffer fools—lesser men who would climb Sinai, or personify the sanctity of the Tabernacle.

But, I, Moses, the man who would come to climb Sinai turned to anxiety, and later to hatred; and, finally, to overreaction.

But this was an overreaction that God chose to countenance. For although Korah's attack was on me, not God, I knew, as clearly as I would know anything, that God was with me, and that I needed Him to manifest it.

❦

The incapacities of individuals oftimes influence significant moments in the lives of men. And when the men so burdened are, indeed, leaders in the chronicle of mankind, the distresses and painful moments that mold action, or inaction, are not abandoned. They become enlarged by the number of those affected.

Still, the Written Word, and perhaps the history of mankind will only record "result"—not the individual events of men's lives

"The hatred Korah felt against Moses was still more kindled by his wife. When, after the consecration of the Levites, Korah returned home, his wife noticed that the hairs of his head and of his body had been shaved, and asked him who had done all this to him. He answered, 'Moses,' whereupon his wife remarked: 'Moses hates thee and did this to disgrace thee.' Korah, however, replied 'Moses shaved all the hair of his own sons also.' But she said: 'What did the disgrace of his own sons matter to him if he only felt he could disgrace thee? He was quite ready to make that sacrifice.'" (j. Sanhedrin 110a; Legends III)

that sometimes lay at the core of human events and influences result. Pain. Pettiness. Doubt. Fear.

That morning brought pain. My past brought fear.

Fluid stuffed my head. The cadence, the throbbing against my head, was relentless. My bones ached. My stomach was distended with pain. My throat was sore and parched. I couldn't bring myself to leave my tent, and offered my barely audible morning prayers alone, in recline against a cushion.

I lay down again upon completing my prayers, but was awakened by an odd, distant noise. I arose and approached the opening of the tent. In the far distance, I saw an elusive mirage: a sea of blue undulating toward me along the desert floor. It seemed to flow up and down as it crawled toward me over the dunes and berms of the desert terrain. It was a sea of blue that I had not encountered since we stood at the Sea's edge a year before—the moment of His miraculous conquest that had brought down His thunderous tide against the army of Pharaoh, who sought to defy Him.

But I could never have imagined what the tide would bring in this day.

For as the blue sea drew closer and the ripples became more perceptible, I saw that this tide rushed in on scores of marching feet: two hundred and fifty men in all. Each man was a "prince" marching in wholly blue raiment, led by one man. Korah, my frequent enemy of a time gone by, was the only man I would immediately recognize and whose stance would concern me. He was a force who would return from my past to stand in defiance at my doorstop.

As I looked beyond the team of Korah's princes, I could see thousands gathering to listen. As I rubbed the sleep from my eyes, I could see that this was no mirage. Mirages present that for which we long, not that which we instead loathe.

The quickening beat of my heart temporarily repressed the pain that tormented me that morning. But Korah quickly realized that I was not, then, myself—even if I could ever forefend against this accomplished orator. For he was a skilled user of the twin meaning; a "user" who concealed a dagger in his every verbal offering.

Korah engaged in no superficial salutations. He was simply poised to attack. His attack, though, outwardly seemed an attack on *me*, not on my position. He quickly pointed his finger almost to my chest, and in words curiously not

"What did Korah do [after hearing the law of fringes]? He went and made some garments that were completely dyed blue. Then he went to Moses and said: Moses our teacher, is a garment that is already completely blue nonetheless obliged to have the [blue corner] fringes? He said: It is…Whereupon Korah said: the Torah is not of divine origin, and Moses is not a prophet and Aaron is not the high priest."
(j. Sanhedrin 10:1, Legends III)

mentioned in the Written Word he demanded: "If a garment is all blue, must the garment also contain a fringe of blue thread at its corner?" (He referred to the commandment that we wear fringes and a blue thread on the corner of our shawls and cloaks.)

As no mountain was nearby to lend added sound to his voice, the rear numbers of Korah's throng could surely not hear his question. Nor could his voice have been audible to the multitude that had gathered to follow his procession.

They, as I, though, could perceive, despite the outward innocence of the inquiry, the challenging affect with which it was asked. For that reason, the emerging approval of Korah that became louder in the din of those assembled deafened me. And it deafened Aaron, too, who had come to my tent, at first seemingly mindless of the emerging attacks.

Looking back, Korah's questions themselves—more would follow—were hardly defiant, nor, at first, outwardly disrespectful to God or His Command. They were the contents of a believer's dialogue. But Korah would not digest or even listen to any answer from me. He, instead, posed, in rapid succession, other questions: "Can one rob from the poor?" There was no clear harm in that question. But, again, he had no time or desire for an answer.

The din would roar again, although they could not even hear his question. All they could perceive was a distant stance of defiance, and the slouching response by an aging, defenseless Moses, clearly overcome by the tremors of a sickly man—a man who, in Korah's phrase, had taken on "too much," exalting himself over the Congregation of God. Was my reaction to Korah caused by the personalizing of his attack on me? My personal disgust notwithstanding, however, anyone, at least anyone who stood in my sandals that day, would have seen Korah's plot for what it was. Plainly, he was not there to hear or digest answers, nor even to probe. He was there just to provoke, and assume a stance of rebellion against the force of a despot that he perceived me to be. He posed a stance against one who presumed to secure God's Holy Mantle for himself and his brother in the supposed Name of God. It didn't matter that he had also defamed me.

It was his manipulation, his defiance—the unmistakable marching of a blue throng to my door. This was no act of chance, but of deliberate confrontation; not of talmudic dialogue, but of rebellious insurrection. The blue raiments, and what they represented, had become the uniform of an attacking enemy. The sickness that I experienced that day did not so pervert my ability to perceive what was at hand. Korah did not come to my tent in discovery of the difficulties of God's Commandments.

Still, did I need to call on God to destroy Korah so boldly as I did? Was my reaction unduly influenced by his attacks in our youth, or of that day? Or both? Or was it simply because the multitude could witness that my rival had again reduced me to a stammerer, who still could not defend God's commands in an encounter with a challenger of noble pose. It was a reminder of the weakness that I showed Pharaoh.

God came to my side that day, I believe, because I needed Him to. In mankind's terms, I had unwittingly forced His hand, lest I be reduced in the eyes of his people. I had somehow provoked a duel with Korah, from which, without God's aid, I would lie in defeat. It was not because He concluded that Korah's destruction was needed for His Divine purpose, but because God sometimes, *if only sometimes,* will stand behind those He has chosen, as He did that day.

The Children of Israel will easily remember what happened to Korah and his followers that fateful day. It is there in black and white. But they will take little note, and soon forget, the mystery that encapsules His pity: a pity for those whose individual destinies, whether fathomable or not, are needed, finally, to His plan.

But what is most important in all that happened that day must be remembered: Korah's sons saw the encounter for what it was, and, without showing disrespect for their father, resolved not to follow his way. They lived, instead, to sing the praises of God.

It would be my fervent wish that their psalms be firmly remembered; that their identity as psalmists be invoked in every generation to teach one lesson: Every man, no matter his birth or rearing, may leave the path of waywardness to pursue a better direction in righteousness' name.

Chapter 16
The Rock

*The Israelites, the whole congregation, came into
the wilderness of Zin in the first month, and the
people stayed in Kadesh. Miriam died there, and
was buried there. Now there was no water for the
congregation; so they gathered together against
Moses and against Aaron. The people quarreled
with Moses and said, "Would that we had died
when our kindred died before the LORD! Why
have you brought the assembly of the LORD into
this wilderness for us and our livestock to die
here?..." The LORD spoke to Moses, saying: Take
the staff, and assemble the congregation, you and
your brother Aaron, and command the rock
before their eyes to yield its water. Thus you shall
bring water out of the rock for them; thus you
shall provide drink for the congregation and
their livestock. So Moses took the staff from
before the LORD, as he had commanded him.*

Moses and Aaron gathered the assembly together before the rock, and he said to them, "Listen, you rebels, shall we bring water for you out of this rock?" Then Moses lifted up his hand and struck the rock twice with his staff; water came out abundantly, and the congregation and their livestock drank. (Num 20:1–4, 7–11)

But the LORD said to Moses and Aaron, "Because you did not trust in me, to show my holiness before the eyes of the Israelites, therefore you shall not bring this assembly into the land that I have given them." (Num 20:12)

Does a sighted man know what it means to be blind, or a virgin the bodily pleasure of marital relations? Can those who have never truly hungered know the pain of starvation?

Can humans who have never lacked water comprehend the true meaning of "thirst?" Can they feel the dry parched feeling on the mouth and tongue, day after day; the pounding pains; the body's drying up and clamping in odious pain; the all-consuming need for water of any kind, even if already used or infested? Have they seen false images on the desert floor that make one believe that there is a pond in the distance, when all that exists is a tantalizing, apparition looming over the sand? Can they understand how relief for this craving will not come soon—if ever?

For a person so consumed, nothing else matters—save a belief that life before "the Thirst," however miserable, was still better. That is the plain they reached. They considered bodily torture; loss of freedom; the raping of women; murder of first-born males; slavery's humiliation—all, astonishingly, preferable to "the Thirst." A people so tormented become more akin to animals than men.

Will those who follow us ever fully grasp, without equal pain, what was truly at stake at the Waters of Meribah (and before that, at Rephidim)? Will they realize that we had been reduced to the plane of animals, and conducted ourselves as they would? Will our descendants be showing true virtue to criticize those who suffered as did these people—not having walked the desert in the sandals that we wore while traveling toward to thirst and desiccation. *How, then, could I myself have made such judgments of them?*

I concluded that God did truly appreciate "human thirst," having remained calm when the people so harshly complained over water. Both at Rephidim and then at Meribah, He seemed undisturbed by them, even when they attacked me for taking them from Egypt.

Perhaps, then, it is evident why he was distressed by me at Meribah and, thus, denied Aaron, who was blameless there, and I the Promised Land. Plainly, I was unjustified in rebuking the Hebrews, when I called them "rebels," when perhaps because I was distracted with the work of the Lord, I more easily dealt with the Thirst. So—was it my anger?

But was my "anger" so terribly at odds with God's Image I had come to know? Did God, the Ultimate Empath, not previously threaten the people's annihilation when they were faithless to Him in the desert? But, still, even though I surely lacked restraint, would He be seen as vengeful to punish me with death as we neared the Jordan for having been vengeful?

Was it, then, because I hit the rock, rather than speak to it and, thus, detracted from His miracle? Did I lead the Children of Israel to falsely conclude that in striking the rock I unleashed an underground well of water, when merely "talking" to the rock would have been more miraculous? It is not likely—even for an exacting God.

Was God annoyed that I said: "O rebels, shall *we* bring forth water to you from this rock?"—falsely leading them to conclude that Aaron and I, not God, were the true miracle workers? Unlikely again.

The belief that God was offended by my innocent action in hitting the rock that "diminished" His miracle, or my wrongful use of words that suggested that *we*, instead, produced the water, is odd. Was God so petty, needing to prove Himself to these pathetic slaves that He alone had liberated? Are such the judgments of the God I worship?

Those who would explain God's reason for the death that awaits me today, reduce God's magnificence with such mortal man reasons for His actions.

❦

In my lonely thinking back on my life, I wonder if God ever smiles. And, if so, I wonder if He will smile when I say that I never believed that hitting the rock, or accepting credit for the miracle, or becoming provoked with the Israelites, was the reason why I was denied the Promised Land.

God knew my many faults, first seen by Him at the Burning Bush. But by the time we reached the Wilderness of Zin, after all that had occurred, He could no longer have doubted my belief or, for that reason alone, have been motivated to deny me.

Is it relevant that God announced my fate and that of Aaron to die in the Wilderness shortly after "the Rock"? Does that which precedes cause? Did my actions at the Rock cause the punishment for Aaron and me that He announced at that point in time?

No, the Rock, to me, is like a final straw that forces a camel to the ground from a burgeoning load. It was the piling upon the camel's back of sins, weaknesses and mistakes in which I failed to "sanctify" God in the Desert. There was my unfaithfulness at the Burning Bush; my failure to leap boldly into the Red Sea; my destruction of the First Tablets; my conduct with the Spies; and, finally, the Rock. The Rock, in my mind's eye, symbolized all my failures.

But there is something more—far more.

I realized thirty-nine years ago, long before the Waters of Meribah, that I would never reach the Promised Land. Some say

I sinned in lacking faith, when I initially dispatched the fated spies. That incident, however, must, for a moment, be put aside.

Conjure, instead, the image of a ship pilot who, with great hope, orders his ship to sea. He alone is focused on foreboding skies predicting storm at the horizon. Once at sea, he commands his oarsmen to row harder seemingly into the storm's oncoming, ferocious squalls. His men, though, all the grown men of the fishing village, lack the bravery to persevere, in spite of the pilot's warnings. In calamity, in refusal to adopt the faith of their pilot, they fall into the sea n'er to be seen again. The heroic efforts of the pilot to save them are in vain. In the irony of the maelstrom, the squalls save the pilot who never lifted an oar. He survives, washed ashore to a safety never reached by any of his oarsmen.

The pilot's lifetime history of brave passage is extolled. But in his return he is doomed to forever walk in shadow and misery in the fated village of his embarkation. Survival for this pilot, who called men to the sea from a position of uncompromising faith in the Divine Wind Blower, is cursed.

Better it would have been for the pilot, too, to have died at sea, lest he drown in the recriminating undertow of the widows and orphans of his hapless crew—or, worse, still, the undertow of a guilty inner voice. The "appearance" of Divine fairness sometimes must prevail over a "just" result.

So, too, here, for God to have allowed thousands of Israelites to die on this side of the Jordan for accepting the Spies' faithless account, but allow Aaron and I to cross, may have been a just result. It would be, though, desperately flawed by the appearance of partiality, without a sense of virtue. There resulted an exquisite clash in competing Divine Attributes that, I always recognized, would *righteously* make me a pilot who must die at sea with his crew.

Chapter 17
Interludes

[Moses said] "Give ear, O heavens, and I will speak; let the earth hear the words of my mouth. May my teaching drop like the rain, my speech condense like the dew; like gentle rain on grass, like showers on new growth. For I will proclaim the name of the LORD; ascribe greatness to our God! The Rock, his work is perfect, and all his ways." (Deut 32:1–3)

Moses came and recited all the words of this song in the hearing of the people, he and Joshua son of Nun. When Moses had finished reciting all these words to all Israel, he said to them: "Take to heart all the words that I am giving in witness against you today; give them as a command to your children, so that they may diligently observe all the

words of this law. This is no trifling matter for
you, but rather your very life; through it you
may live long in the land that you are crossing
over the Jordan to possess."

(Deut 32:44–47)

Months passed since the plague killed the ten spies, and the people had learned that their lot was to wander aimlessly in a desert—nomads who would never reach a homeland.

But the deaths of the spies and those who rushed into defeat against Amalek seeking to repent, yielded surprising relief. The relief of finality—knowing one's fate, as preferable to the obscure satan of the unknown.

It reminded me of my time back in Egypt. I sometimes listened, there, to an itinerant wiseman who wandered in the shadows along the outer corridors of the palace. He told a tale of a journey through the netherworld by a long-deceased ancestor of Pharaoh, a hero in the folklore of Egypt. During his journey, he beheld a figure known to the Egyptians as Sofian—a man condemned to suffer a deplorable decree in the netherworld, for his reckless rebellion to the enemy gods.

Sofian's solitary lot was to paddle his stone-laden boat endlessly against the overpowering currents of the Nile until exhaustion just as his densely heavy boat would approach the far side of the river. And just before the moment of reaching his destination, the nostrils of the enemy gods would blow a strenuous wind to instantaneously drive his boat back across the river. The wind would surge almost spontaneously to render worthless the exhausting effort that had consumed Sofian's existence. His lot? To renew his journey, again; then, hopelessly exhausted, to fail to reach his destination across the river. To begin. To fail again. Again and again, throughout Eternity.

The Egyptians saw Sofian as a wretched figure, ensnared in the painful struggle against one's destiny, a timeless figure reborn in every generation, but doomed each time. He was a figure who would be transfigured in the lore of every people: a figure in endless despair.

To the dissident wiseman in Pharaoh's court, though, Sofian was not a man in despair. Sofian, for him, was happy. He was a man who alone knew his fate and possessed it—even at that tortured moment when, in an instant, his boat (and life) would be blown back across the river.

But, I never accepted the wiseman's view of Sofian: knowing one's fate is worthless when one knows that one's struggle will be purposeless.

The Israelites, after their sin with the spies, knew their fate—a wandering existence that would only end at death. But comparing them to Sofian ended there.

Their fate had a compelling purpose. Surely, the repulsive, wanderer's life was not eased knowing that an aimless wandering would yield nothing better in their lifetime. But, unlike Sofian, they knew that their destiny was purposeful—to enable their children's stake in the Promised Land. It was a price they had to pay, the suffering they willingly endured for what was truly their own future, writ large on the smiling faces of the "unshackled."

Atop Sinai, I had listened intently as He delivered the words I was to inscribe. It was lost on me, how purposefully His Book withheld nuance and detail. The gradations and the trivial. The private and the unprofound.

My solitary moments, my private thoughts, would remain my own. My times or thoughts between the moments of anguish and those of rapture lack posterity. The seemingly insignificant events in my life will be buried today, along with me. This pleases me greatly now that I realize His Plan.

He told me what came before; but despite the insight He gave me, I yearned to know so much more.

How did Noah deal, daily, with the aloneness of his faith? How did he remain unmoved—if he did—to the barbs hurled at him as he built his vessel to save man?

What were the solitary thoughts of Abraham when alone—without a hatchet in his hand poised to destroy the idols of his father, Terah, to prove they were useless, or to sacrifice his son Isaac to prove his love for God? Could his faith have been so uncompromising at every moment, while climbing Moriah? Was there clandestine laughter or glee? Or was there disabling grief during Abraham's journey that we will never read about?

What inner torment coursed through Isaac when Abraham's faith seemed to drive him so close to killing him? Did

Isaac secretly wonder, later, whether the test was too weighty, and seek the nonbeliever's moments of noise or frivolity? Or did he simply later laugh about a fleeting, youthful painful moment, soothed, then, by the distance traveled since?

Did Jacob secretly repent his zealotry for blessings that seemed, to some, so questionable in the way in which he received them. Did he later silently wonder why Joseph had never sent him news of his survival or successes in those many years before Joseph's brothers came to Egypt, suffering from famine, only to reconcile with Joseph instead? Did Jacob address the personal grief he suffered by drunkenness, or by private acts of charity that we will never know? Or was he, instead, gratified to have been punished—to earn absolution for past offense?

Did Joseph's faith endure, at every moment, in his turmoil? Or did the humanness of revenge, or ironic acts of private sinfulness, overtake him in the dungeon of Potiphar, after being falsely accused of raping the viceroy's wife? Were there moments when he dropped out from the crucible of integrity in which his parents raised him?

I thought as I asked myself these questions—is it only I who has suffered doubt, or reneged on belief?

Or, lest I be consumed with the dooming fact of today's ending, is it just I who yearned, sometimes, for "the trifling"—

"...Esau said to Jacob, 'Let me eat some of that red stuff, for I am famished!' (Therefore he was called Edom.) Jacob said, 'First sell me your birthright.' Esau said, 'I am about to die; of what use is a birthright to me?' Jacob said, 'Swear to me first.' So he swore to him, and sold his birthright to Jacob. Then Jacob gave Esau bread and lentil stew, and he ate and drank, and rose and went his way. Thus Esau despised his birthright." (Gen 25:29–34)

a romp with my grandchildren in oasis grass just rained on? Or is it I alone who enjoyed a daily sunset to gaze at with Zipporah's hand in mine—unconcerned that my flock would see me pursuing a selfish trifling? Is there no one else who yearned for a month of Sabbaths to forget the head pains of being a constant "protector" for so many. Did those who came before me likewise yearn for the simple aroma of a bed of flowers?

So many questions, but so few insights—except for those who allow their imaginations to breathe life into the arable interludes of timeless moments in the lives of men, which the Written Torah leaves incomplete.

I wanted to learn the hard and the fast of those moments, to apply what came before for myself. I sought to learn, for imitation in my life, from the undaunted exemplars of time gone by. I wanted so to almost be Noah, Abraham, Isaac, Jacob and Joseph—the warriors against self-doubt and disillusion. I yearned to represent their undescribed moments in His name.

"[T]he men who brought an unfavorable report about the land died by a plague before the LORD. But Joshua son of Nun and Caleb son of Jephunneh alone remained alive, of those men who went to spy out the land." (Num 14:37–38)

But it was not to be. Our lives are ours. The Torah provides the pillars of the structure to fashion our lives. We, alone, are the artisans who must fill the spaces between. Even the possibility of adornment by strict imitation would deny the preciousness of freedom to choose our own paths—the foundation of our being.

The furor over the spies died down. The spies themselves, excepting Joshua and Caleb, quickly died in a plague. And those who, too late, chose to enter Canaan, despite my contrary urging, were killed by the Amelikites.

Time passed. The people became resigned to a lifelong wandering existence in the Wilderness. Surprisingly, while that existence was not ideal, the people became comforted in their plight. For despite their frequent murmurs saying otherwise, they had never, realistically, known a better life in Egypt. Ironically, only I, who grew up in Pharaoh's palace, and the many Egyptians who joined us in the Exodus, knew a better existence. To be sure, the poor don't recognize their poverty, nor recognize their discomfiture— unless they were once comfortable. I, curiously, the only one who knew better, had no time to recall, to concentrate on the luxuries or comforts I now lacked: a jewel-encrusted robe, or a soothing bath, followed by a rub of my shoulders to help relieve the day's pains.

*"Never since has there arisen a prophet in Israel like Moses, whom the L*ORD* knew face to face. He was unequaled for all the signs and wonders that the L*ORD* sent him to perform in the land of Egypt, against Pharaoh and all his servants and his entire land, and for all the mighty deeds and all the terrifying displays of power that Moses performed in the sight of all Israel."*
(Deut 34:10–12)

The secrecy of my thoughts remain that way for those moments when I laid my staff aside and became at one with my fellow wanderers of such large number. The pangs of hunger; the caprice of the daydream; the aches caused by rejection; the light-heartedness inspired by a baby's smile, or, the melody plucked by a soothing harpist, will nowhere be revealed.

But private moments were not easily gained by me. I resisted accepting the well-meaning persuasions of Jethro, to appoint judges to address the seemingly trivial quarrels and clashes; the disagreements and dissensions between man and his neighbor; the discords common to every people.

The reluctance to let another carry your water, no matter how confident you may be in the height of his pottery or the steadiness of his hand is a flaw that will surely be repeated in the generations to follow. But my reluctance to yield responsibility was not from lack of trust in my aides.

Rather, once we yielded to wander, my unwillingness to delegate was essentially an act of self-indulgence. The greatest pleasure in my life was to arbitrate and mediate.

My pleasure was not to rule; not to *order* my fellow man to reimburse his neighbor when the latter's ox was gored. The pleasure, lay, instead, in *persuading* my fellow. I enjoyed, within myself, the exhilarating moment when adversarial contact yields to the noble understanding of "duty." I yearned to observe the Israelite undertake with happiness to compensate his fellow when he accepted fault for the damage done by his ox. I resisted as would anyone, abandoning the happiness in seeing, time and again, my fellow man to take within himself the rule of law. But Jethro was right. I could not "do it all."

I found, though, a secret way to continue this pleasure I so coveted. I would walk among the people, and talk with them. I would let them "self-persuade"—not because Moses told them what to do, but having been at Sinai, they, within themselves, knew what was proper.

The weekday allowed no time to traverse the camp, and the mask that covered my face since Sinai was too inhibiting to them. On the Sabbath, though, I was like any other—my face's "radiance" that I never myself perceived, disappeared. All of Israel was on the same plain—no need for a mask to protect them from embarrassment.

Thus, I would walk to the far reaches of the camp—the epitome of pleasureful "rest" that was commanded by God for the Sabbath day. I would use the walk, not encumbered by the escort that customarily surrounded me, to learn the people's travails and, in simple dialogue, let them subject themselves to His law.

I was for them a simple reflecting pool, not a dignitary imposing law. These were the private moments that touched me more than any in my life. I walked as one among equals, and relished the simple accomplishments that otherwise escaped me.

There is no mask or need of one, when there is a complete acceptance of His rule.

The rule of judging that compels me most is that when the judging is completed and both parties accept the decision, both parties are without fault—even the wrongdoer. The wrongdoer is especially innocent, when he recognizes his fault.

These were my private moments. Here is where I was at a peace never described in His Torah.

Surely, this was not the way Zipporah intended that I spend my Sabbath—for we were apart so much and I was so distracted in our waking hours. She tried to protect me so, fearing the words of father Jethro: *"Thou will surely wear away…for this thing is too heavy for thee, thou art not able to perform it thyself alone"*— she feared that I would exhaust myself beyond all possibility of repair.

But Zipporah was a woman created in God's image….

Chapter 18
Dusk

Then Moses went up from the plains of Moab to Mount Nebo, to the top of Pisgah, which is opposite Jericho, and the LORD showed him the whole land; Gilead as far as Dan, all Naphtali, the land of Ephraim and Manasseh, all the land of Judah as far as the Western Sea, the Negeb, and the Plain—that is, the valley of Jericho, the city of palm trees—as far as Zoar. The LORD said to him, "This is the land of which I swore to Abraham, to Isaac, and to Jacob, saying, 'I will give it to your descendants'; I have let you see it with your eyes, but you shall not cross over there." Then Moses, the servant of the LORD, died there in the land of Moab,… opposite Beth-peor, but no one knows his burial place to this day. Moses was one hundred twenty years old when he died; his sight was unimpaired and his vigor had not abated. (Deut 34:1–7)

My time has come.

It is like a gentle, but firm tap on my shoulder to tell me I can delay here no longer. Dusk on the end of my Day of Judgment is fleeting quickly into full darkness—the Book of Life has been closed, without my name enscribed. The end is near, but unlike so many others who died before me I am certain of it.

The substitution of this existence—even if He is to find me worthy of a paradise—will not, I fear, allow me the free will to effect His Command. He has said if only with the elusive implicit that we are drifters in what is only a portal leading to the World to Come. Even still, I would opt for an endless such corridor in which to continue. Life in preference to death, no matter what either might hold in store. The satan we know, not the stranger.

But do I, again, lack faith? Do I say this merely to justify my fear of having been condemned to the unknown? After all, the place to where He takes us is unknown, since He offers for that existence only phrases containing hint and implication.

Do I, thus, harbor inner doubt of what will come when the squeaky portal closes behind? And would such confidence in a garden of eden to lie ahead represent an arrogance that would shut the door tight—and forbid entrance to reward, and ensure only its opposite?

Am I damned for being resigned to the reality that He will not soften His heart for me? And, on the other hand, would I be damned to believe that, having merited it, I shall find a better tomorrow, in a better place and time?

So many questions, and so little time. But I knew that this hour was coming for forty years. Would I have found answers to these questions had I focused on them, leaving out all else?

Enough! He takes me elsewhere now. And, though, I could advocate, or implore, or even beg Him repeatedly for my life, as I did for the Israelites so many times before, I will not do that. I cannot do that. Perhaps in some odd, unforeseen, or even mysterious way I now recognize, I have loved them or, if not them, my duty to them, more than life itself.

I cannot allow myself to be a teacher who, when his time came, took to his knees seeking reprieve for himself alone—a reprieve founded only on self-concern.

Better that I go silently, wrapped now in the appearance of indifference when the moment of death arrives, to better teach them, than be allowed to linger more, and let myself indeed become a shrine. For it would be a flawed shrine that would pay honor to the characteristic of self-preoccupation in the manner of the satan.

I must, then, go upward now where He leads me.

It is surprising how the mind allows one to deceive oneself, and makes one a martyr, if only in one's own eyes, by almost believing the loftiness of one's pretense.

For the concordance of my thoughts, even a simple recollection, would show that bare weeks ago, I would so vigorously implore Him by describing the depth and primitiveness of my desire to enter the Land. I prayed *"voeschanan,"* a kind of prayer I never used before, shamelessly pleading for a special and undeserved favor to see the Land. It was a soulful eruption from within, brewing for forty years within my very being.

Indeed, so soon before I would use the zealotry of my words to propel me across the Jordan—employing my warlike defeats of the kingdom of Og and Sihon, King of Heshbon. Those words were not incantations of a man profoundly dedicated to his wards, as I deluded myself just moments ago, but rather the "elegant" ploy of a man wading in personal desire. In using these words, I suggested, if ever so subtly, that "I deserve it."

Moses! Do you lack shame even in talking to yourself?

Darkness, quickening with every moment, begins to envelop me as the journey's end nears. I look back over my shoulder to see if there is still sunlight in which to stay back for another moment of His warmth. But it is even darker in the direction from which I have come. There is no turning back.

A strange force pushes my hand down on the head of my staff and forces my body to stand. It draws me to the top of the Mountain, which looks to the west—a site of yet another miracle. For despite the blackness to the east in my past and the darkness that increasingly immerses the place where I stand, the sun still burns brightly across the cliff to the west. And while I can see nothing that immediately surrounds me, I see clearly in the distant west across the Jordan.

Is it because the sun is there, or because my heart is in the west? I briefly forget that darkness surrounds me, and that I have reached the end of my journey. And though I am momentarily tortured in renewed hope for myself by the panorama of what I see, I soon forget my self-concern when I realize what He shows me.

It is not that He shows me a beauteous land—for Egypt, too, was beauteous. Nor that He shows me Jericho and Gilead and Judah, as far as the western sea. And the Negev. And Hebron where Abraham is buried, or Bethlehem where Rachel lies. Or even that He shows me the beautiful orchards on the Mount of Olives, from which place the righteous will each ascend on the final Day of Judgment.

But it is that He lets me *see* tomorrow—whether I see it in my eye; in my mind's eye; or in my heart. For, in one luminous moment, He lets me see that this journey was not in vain. That we traversed the mountains and valleys, and endured the torture of combat and humiliating slavery, all for a glorious purpose. It is that purpose that I see in the distance.

It is, too, not because I see the vineyards of figs and dates, and pomegranates and olives. But, because I see children playing and men working in those vineyards, in the warm sunlight of their future. It is a future that lies only to the west.

I, thus, have indeed now crossed the Jordan, and, in some indescribable way, the bodily restraint that He has imposed on me in my race against death no longer matters, because I have come to inhabit the Land.

❧

The images remain clear and bright. But my eyes are fixed at the place, where He told me He created the world, Mount Moriah—just beside the Mount of Olives. It is the place where Abraham would accept the ultimate challenge of his faith and offer to sacrifice his son Isaac. It is where, in recognition of Abraham's unvacillating commitment to God, the Temple will one day stand.

As my eyes are fixed on the Temple Mount, however, I see an odd cloud atop it. I see tomorrow, but a blur that makes me uncertain of it. Amidst that sunbathed spot in the distance from which the rising smoke and frankincense of sacrifice waft upwards, I see men dressed in one nation's battle armor, then another's—carrying swords marching toward the Temple.

I cry out to let the Priests and Levites know that there are armed men poised to attack from the Temple courtyard. But they cannot hear me. My wails are from a future past.

It is not the distance in space or time that deafens them to my warnings. It is that our successors must learn the danger that awaits them for themselves. We may warn our children and our children's children to be wary of the Amalekites of this world and the other satans that they will encounter, but we cannot be their night watchmen through their lifetimes.

The enemies lurk inward from the far side of the Temple, and as the moments pass they come closer into view. I am uncertain of their origin. Are they truly men dressed in the armor of the Canaanite, the Philistine, the Amalekite or other enemies? Or are they simply armored attackers garbed in the evil motive and thoughtless slander of the Israelite against his brother? *Does the enemy lie within us?*

Or is something else at stake? There is no doubt as to the infallibility of His Plan. Still, He has decided before and presumably will again that all of His creations must suffer. And hard as that may be to accept, it is not ours to comprehend why—any more than why four hundred years ago He decided that the Children of Abraham would be enslaved perhaps for sins that long preceded them.

Sadly, the people whom I have led, by action or inaction, by direction or indirection, may have added to the attack I see to the west. And it may be that the attack upon them may stem from our "conquest" of the Land, and His decision that we realize our inheritance. For a "Holy War"—and, surely, a holy war it will be, however Divinely authored and well-intentioned—will leave the sons and daughters, grandchildren and great grandchildren of the defeated, to seek revenge for deeds gone by. As, indeed, we are ordered in the wake of the battle against or by Amalek, perhaps there is a holy war that will have been "ordered" at the instance of the pagan god to which the Amalekites bow.

Some will say that *our* Holy War was just, having been ordered by God, and theirs is not because a pagan idol made by man "ordered" it. But still, those pagans listen to that god and believe in it. Consider what it took for Pharaoh and his wise men to recognize *our* God. And did they recognize Him even then?

"[A]nd one of them, a lawyer, asked him a question to test him. 'Teacher, which commandment in the law is the greatest?' He said to him, 'You shall love the Lord your God with all your heart, and with all your soul, and with all your mind.' This is the greatest and first commandment. And a second is like it: "You shall love your neighbor as yourself.' On these two commandments hang all the law and the prophets." (Matt 22:35–40)

As I look across the cliffs, I see that it may well be that we will have to kill—for "conquest" means killing—the Canaanites, the Hittites, the Amorites, the Perezites and others; we must do so lest our children stray to the pagan gods to whom those nations bow.

But when we kill them, and purge them, and anathematize them, and perhaps we must, rather than make ourselves exemplars of man's righteousness under the regime of God, they may repeat the murders against us—if not tomorrow, in tomorrow's tomorrow.

Instead, we must "kill" and purge and anathematize all that is wrong with us—thus to avoid the need for conquest or the allure of straying. We must enforce good conduct that will deny the pagan altar any quarter in our homes, and, thereby, become models for the true meaning of "chosen."

One is not "chosen" by his ancestry. He is chosen by the way he conducts himself—if, like Noah, he walks with God, not because he tells the stranger that he is entitled, by happenstance of birth, to God's grace. Envy is a weed not to be watered.

A warm breeze begins to blow from west to east. Momentarily, I close my eyes to protect them from the swirling sands, ever fearful at this late moment that my eyes, once closed, will never reopen. I am fearful that the oasis to the west will remain eternally beneath a cloud of foreboding, and pain—a cloud of injustice and inequity; of vengeful neighbors, and unrealized dreams. A land of "promise," but without fulfillment—where, too frequently, the good die young—many, in seeming innocence.

But when the wind subsides my eyes quickly reopen. My head reflexively turns from east to west. From east to west; and then again. From darkness to light; and then again. The darkest of dark becomes again a prelude to the morning light—when all shattered dreams are once again realizable. It is the morning light when everything becomes, again, clear with the promise that lies to the west.

And I come to see that life is like that, for people go from light to darkness, and back again. That men or people without faults are apt to be men or people without force. A round diamond has no brilliance. Lights and shadows, hills and valleys, give beauty to the landscape. The faults of great and generous natures are overripe goodness, or the shadows that their virtues cast.

Those Israelites in the distance will surely have their flaws. And many will suffer dearly in prelude to their rebirth, and in anticipation of resurrection. Some will need to surrender to their enemies, or fall by the wayside in pestilence—just as we have, so often, along this path.

As the clouds disperse in the distance, though, I see that despite the twists and turns along the way, at the End of Days the Israelites will be true to Him and the Destiny that is His "promise." More than that, I can offer little.

But to lose faith before that day's arrival, even though He tarries, is to lose oneself in the darkness and ignore, or even spurn, the coming light. It is the light of the sun that He alone created, and that has risen on every day since time began. It is the sun that will rise tomorrow in the east, just as surely as the darkness covers it now.

Like a tender kiss from my beloved, I feel His warm breath upon me. The temporal darkness finally engulfs me. My words come harder, and I stammer as before. Still, through what He has shown to me, I am finally a servant at peace—at peace with himself and with His Master, and all that He has offered me.

For better than letting me to walk with my people in the Promised Land, He has indulged me to see the beauty and magnificence of His continuum, and how, despite all, He has loved them so. And He has shown me how He, too, has suffered, as does any parent whose child goes astray, requiring the parent's remonstration as an act of love. But one thing I know as surely as I have ever known anything: that "they"—not they who have been chosen, but they who have willingly made the choice—will both recognize and accept the encounter that awaits them.

And that one day, with the grace of God, I will again walk among them in Him. Not I, Moses. But Moses, the son of Amram—just another simple man, a timid servant of the Lord, who walks quietly among God's People.

Reflections on Moses
after His Death

*M*oses: *A Memoir* tries to create a sense of the inner feelings and deeply religious convictions that Moses must have experienced in his eventful life, which included a long and difficult mission directed by God's purposes. For modern people, curiosity about the interior thoughts and struggles of our heroes is very strong and invites such spiritual reflection as this book portrays. But ancients were also greatly impressed by the person of Moses and often meditated on his accomplishments and sometimes even filled in the holes in their knowledge about his life with a variety of legends and inspirational stories. Because all of these accounts, whether sober or speculative, reveal the great respect that our long-ago ancestors in faith had for Moses, it is valuable to provide some samples of their writings in the following pages. The passages are chosen from the Scriptures and a variety of Jewish and Christian writings that date between 200 B.C.E. and 500 C.E.

Psalm 90, in tradition composed by Moses himself, reminds us that the swift passing of man's stay on earth would make it meaningless, were it not that God is everlasting and under Him is man's abiding dwelling place:

A Prayer of Moses the Man of God

Lord, you have been our dwelling place in all generations. Before the mountains were brought forth, or ever you had formed the earth and the world, from everlasting to everlasting you are God. You turn us back to dust, and say, "Turn back, you mortals." For a thousand years in your sight are like yesterday when it is past, or like a watch in the night. You sweep them away; they are like a dream, like grass that is renewed in the morning; in the morning it flourishes and is renewed; in the evening it fades and withers.

(Ps 90:1–6)

Chapter 4: The Burning Bush

Some Sadducees, who say there is no resurrection, came to him and asked him a question, saying, "Teacher, Moses wrote for us that if a man's brother dies, leaving a wife but no child, the man shall marry the widow and raise up children for his brother. There were seven brothers; the first married and, when he died, left no children; and the second married her and died, leaving no children; and the third likewise; none of the seven left children. Last of all the woman herself died. In the resurrection whose wife will she be? For the seven had married her."

Jesus said to them, "Is not this the reason you are wrong, that you know neither the scriptures nor the power of God? For when they rise from the dead, they neither marry nor are given in marriage, but are like angels in heaven. And as for the dead being raised, have you not read in the book of Moses, in the story about the bush, how God said to him, 'I am the God of Abraham, the God of Isaac, and the God of Jacob'? He is God not of the dead, but of the living; you are quite wrong."   (Mark 12:18–27)

Chapter 6: The Ten Plagues

Psalm 105 is a retrospective to God's dealings with Abraham and his descendants, including Moses:

Then Israel came to Egypt; Jacob lived as an alien in the land of Ham. And the LORD made his people very fruitful, and made them stronger than their foes, whose hearts he then turned to hate his people, to deal craftily with his servants. He sent his servant Moses, and Aaron whom he had chosen. They performed his signs among them, and miracles in the land of Ham. He sent darkness, and made the land dark; they rebelled against his words. He turned their waters into blood, and caused their fish to die. Their land swarmed with frogs, even in the chambers of their kings. He spoke, and there came swarms of flies, and gnats throughout their country. He gave them hail for rain, and lightning that flashed through their land. He struck their vines and fig trees, and shattered the trees of their country. He spoke, and the locusts came, and young locusts without number; they devoured all the vegetation in their land, and ate up the fruit of their ground. He struck down all the firstborn in their land, the first issue of all their strength. Then he brought Israel out with silver and gold, and there was no one among their tribes who stumbled. Egypt was glad when they departed, for dread of them had fallen upon it.

(Ps 105:23–38)

Chapter 7: The Sea of Reeds

By faith Abraham, when put to the test, offered up Isaac. He who had received the promises was ready to offer up his only son, of whom he had been told, "It is through Isaac that descendants shall be named for you." He considered the fact that God is able even to raise someone from the dead—and figuratively speaking, he did receive him back. By faith Isaac invoked blessings for the future on Jacob and Esau. By faith Jacob, when dying, blessed each of the sons of Joseph, "bowing in worship over the top of his staff." By

faith Joseph, at the end of his life, made mention
of the exodus of the Israelites and gave instruc-
tions about his burial. By faith Moses was hidden by his parents for three months after his
birth, because they saw that the child was beautiful; and they were not afraid of the king's edict.
By faith Moses, when he was grown up, refused
to be called a son of Pharaoh's daughter, choos-
ing rather to share ill-treatment with the people
of God than to enjoy the fleeting pleasures of
sin. He considered abuse suffered for the Christ
to be greater wealth than the treasures of Egypt,
for he was looking ahead to the reward. By faith
he left Egypt, unafraid of the king's anger; for he
persevered as though he saw him who is invisible. By faith he kept the Passover and the sprinkling of blood, so that the destroyer of the
firstborn would not touch the firstborn of Israel.
By faith the people passed through the Red Sea
as if it were dry land, but when the Egyptians
attempted to do so they were drowned.

(Heb 11:17–29)

Chapter 8: The Decalogue

Philo remarks that the human intellect cannot conceive the
essence of God, but only His activities. These remarks attributed
to God in communication with Moses, assists mankind's understanding of Him:

It was the seventh time that He appeared on earth, and taking the guise of a precentor of a congregation, He said to Moses: "Whenever Israel hath sinned, and calleth Me by the following thirteen attributes, I will forgive them their sins. I am the Almighty God who provides for all creatures. I am the Merciful One who restrains evil from human kind. I am the Gracious One who helps in time of need. I am the Long-Suffering to the upright as well as to the wicked. I am Bountiful to those whose own deed do not entitle them to lay claim to rewards. I am Faithful to those who have a right to expect good from Me; and preserve graciousness unto the two-thousandth generation. I forgive misdeeds and even atrocious actions, in forgiving those who repent."

(PRE 46; PR 10, 37b; Sifra;
Roshha-Shanah 17b; Legends III)

Chapter 9: Atop Sinai

Some Pharisees came, and to test him they asked, "Is it lawful for a man to divorce his wife?" He answered them, "What did Moses command you?" They said, "Moses allowed a man to write a certificate of dismissal and to divorce her." But Jesus said to them, "Because of your hardness of heart he wrote this commandment for you. But from the beginning of creation, 'God made them male and female.' 'For this reason a man shall leave his father and mother and be joined to his wife, and the two shall become one flesh.' So they are no longer two, but one flesh. Therefore what God has joined together, let no one separate."

Then in the house the disciples asked him again about this matter. He said to them, "Whoever divorces his wife and marries another commits adultery against her." (Mark 10:2–11)

It is not as though the word of God had failed. For not all Israelites truly belong to Israel, and not all of Abraham's children are his true descendants; but "It is through Isaac that descendants shall be named for you." This means that it is not the children of the flesh who are the children of God, but the children of the promise are counted as descendants. For this is what the promise said, "About this time I will return and Sarah shall have a son." Nor is that all; something similar happened to Rebecca when she had conceived children by one husband, our ancestor Isaac. Even before they had been born or had done anything good or bad (so that God's purpose of election might continue, not by works but by his call) she was told, "The elder shall serve the younger." As it is written, "I have loved Jacob, but I have hated Esau."

What then are we to say? Is there injustice on God's part? By no means! For he says to Moses, "I will have mercy on whom I have mercy, and I will have compassion on whom I have compassion." (Rom 9:6–15)

Chapter 10: The Golden Calf

This legend that tells the reader that Aaron was, indeed, the elect, despite his flaws at the Golden Calf, and links the rod he used to the Messianic future of Israel:

God in His kindness now desired the people once and for all to be convinced of the truth that Aaron was the elect, and his house the house of priesthood, hence he bade Moses convince them in the following fashion. Upon God's command, he took a beam of wood, divided it into twelve rods, bade every prince of a tribe in his own hand write his name on one of the rods respectively, and laid up the rods over night before the sanctuary. Then the miracle came to pass that the rod of Aaron, the prince of the tribe of Levi, bore the Ineffable Name which caused the rod to bloom blossoms over night and to yield ripe almonds....Aaron's rod was then laid up before the Holy Ark by Moses. It was this rod, kings used until the time of the destruction of the Temple, when, in miraculous fashion, it disappeared. Elijah will in the future fetch it forth and hand it over to the Messiah.

(BaR 18.23; Yalkut I, 763; Legends III)

Chapter 16: The Rock

In tradition, Moses was denied the Promised Land for the two reasons described in this legend:

> "I vow that I shall let water flow out of that rock only that I have chosen." He addressed these harsh words not to a few among Israel, but to all the people, for God had brought the miracle to pass that the small space in front of the rock held all Israel. Carried away by anger, Moses still further forgot himself, and instead of speaking to the rock as God had commanded him, he struck a rock chosen by himself. As Moses had not acted according to God's command, the rock did not at once obey, and sent forth only a few drops of water, so that the mockers cried: "Son of Amram, is this for the sucklings and for them that are weaned from the milk?" Moses now waxed angrier still, and for a second time smote the rock, from which gushed streams so mighty that many of his enemies met their death in the

currents, and at the same time water poured out of all the stones and rocks of the desert.

God here upon said to Moses: "Thou and Aaron believed Me not, I forbade you to smite the rock, but thou didst smite it; ye sanctified Me not in the eyes of the children of Israel because ye did not fetch water out of any one of the rocks, as the people wished; ye trespassed against Me when ye said, 'Shall we bring forth water out of this rock?' and ye acted contrary to My command because ye did not speak to the rock as I had bidden ye. I vow, therefore, that 'ye shall not bring this assembly into the land which I have given them,' and not until the Messianic time shall ye two lead Israel to the Holy Land." (BaR 19.19; Tan B IV; 26; Tehillim 78, 345; Legends III)

Chapter 18: Dusk

Chapter opening: Legends aid us to try to capture the last hours and moments of Moses' life, to help us find comfort in our own lives:

On the seventh day of Adar, Moses knew that on this day he should have to die, for a heavenly voice resounded, saying, "Take heed to thyself, O Moses, for thou hast only one more day to live." What did Moses now do? On this day he wrote thirteen scrolls of the Torah, twelve for the twelve tribes, and one he put into the Holy Ark, so that, if they wished to falsify the Torah, the one in the Ark might remain untouched. Moses thought, "If I occupy myself with the Torah, which is the tree of life, this day will draw to a close, and the impending doom will be as naught."

…a voice resounded from heaven, and said to Moses, "Thou hast only five hours more of life." Moses called out to Joshua, "Stay seated like a king before the people!" Then both began to speak before all Israel; Moses read out the text and Joshua expounded. There was no difference of opinion between them, and the words of the two matched like the pearls in a royal crown. But Moses' countenance shone like the sun, and Joshua's like the moon….

In the meanwhile still another hour had passed, and a voice resounded from heaven and said, "Moses, thou hast only one hour more of life!" Moses thereupon said: "O Lord of the world!

Even if Thou wilt not let me enter into the land of Israel, leave me at least in this world, that I may live, and not die." God replied, "If I should not let thee die in this world, how then can I revive thee hereafter for the future world? Thou wouldst, moreover, then give the lie to the Torah, for through thee I wrote therein, "neither is there any that can deliver out of My hand." (Petirat Moshe 122:2, 378; Legends III)

Chapter ending: This tradition tells us that when the time of the righteous—here, Moses—is at an end, their righteousness goes before them, and their reward will be the glory of the Lord:

In the meanwhile Moses' time was at an end. A voice from heaven resounded, saying: "Why, Moses, dost thou strive in vain? Thy last second is at hand." Moses instantly stood up for prayer, and said: "Lord of the world! Be mindful of the day on which Thou didst reveal Thyself to me in the bush of thorns, and be mindful also of the day when I ascended into heaven and during forty days partook of neither food nor drink. Thou, Gracious and Merciful, deliver me not into the hand of Samael." God replied: "I have heard thy prayer. I Myself shall attend to thee and bury thee." Moses now sanctified himself as do the Seraphim that surround the Divine Majesty, whereupon God from the highest heavens revealed Himself to receive Moses' soul. When Moses beheld the Holy One, blessed he His Name, he fell upon his face and said: "Lord of the world! In love didst Thou create the world, and in love Thou guidest it. Treat me also with love, and deliver me not into the hands of the Angel of Death." A heavenly voice sounded and said: "Moses, be not afraid. 'Thy righteousness shall go before thee; the glory of the Lord shall be thy reward.'"

With God descended from heaven three angels, Michael, Gabriel, and Zagzagel. Gabriel arranged Moses' couch, Michael spread upon it a purple garment, and Zagzagel laid down a woolen pillow. God stationed Himself over Moses' head, Michael to his right, Gabriel to his left, and Zagzagel at his feet, whereupon God addressed Moses: "Cross thy feet," and Moses did so. He then said, "Fold thy hands and lay them upon thy breast," and Moses did so. Then God said, "Close thine eyes," and Moses did so. Then God spake to Moses' soul: "My daughter, one hundred and twenty years had I decreed that thou shouldst dwell in this righteous man's body, but hesitate not now to leave it, for thy time is run." (DR 115; 2 Petirat Mosheh 383; Likkutim, V. 169b; Midrash Tannaim 225; Legends III)

Glossary

Abraham. The father of Judaism and monotheism. When Abraham passed God's test and was willing to sacrifice his son Isaac as proof of his love for God, an angel of God told him not to slaughter his son. Instead, he sacrificed a ram that was caught in the thicket atop Mount Moriah (Gen 22:1–17).

Amalek. A nomadic desert nation that gratuitously attacked the Israelites in Rephidim, shortly after the Exodus from Egypt. Joshua, the Israelite military leader defeated Amalek, and God told Moses that He would erase the memory of Amalek (Exod 17:8–16).

Amon Ra. The name of the Egyptian sun god, but not found in the Bible.

Caleb. Son of Jephunneh from the tribe of Judah, was the husband of Miriam, Moses' sister. He was one of the spies sent to spy out the Promised Land. Only he, along with Joshua (son of Nun), returned to report that the Land was good and that Israel should not fear the people of the Land. The Congregation threatened to pelt Caleb and Joshua with stones, and the Lord intervened (Num 14:6–11).

City of Refuge. Moses set aside three cities on the eastern bank of the Jordan where individuals who committed manslaughter (but not murder), received sanctuary from the deceased's next of kin, who could otherwise retaliate against the killer (Num 4:41–43).

Decalogue. Used interchangeably with "The Ten Commandments" (Exod 20). The first statement "I am the LORD your God, who brought you out of the land of Egypt, out of the house of slavery" is not technically a commandment, and, thus, some commentators prefer the word *Decalogue,* which means "ten statements."

Dusk. On Yom Kippur, the yearly Day of Atonement in the Hebrew calendar, the prayer, Ne'ilah, is said at dusk, the last hour of the day (which begins near nightfall). According to tradition, one's name is sealed in the Book of Life for the coming year during the Ne'ilah service. If not so sealed, one is fated for death during that calendar year.

Forefathers or **Patriarchs.** Abraham, his son Isaac and grandson Jacob. Abraham was told by God that his offspring would be "aliens" in a land not their own for four hundred years (Gen 15:13).

High Priest. Appointed to preside over sacrificial worship in the Tabernacle, and later in the Temple in Jerusalem when the Israelites came to the Promised Land. Aaron was the first High Priest and all High Priests and priests were blood descendants of Aaron. A priest is forbidden to be contaminated by dead human bodies. Only the High Priest was permitted to enter the Holy of Holies (the inner sanctum) of the Tabernacle and later the Temple—he would do so on the Day of Atonement to seek absolution for the Congregation (Lev 16).

Holy of Holies. *See* High Priest, *supra.*

Jacob. Grandson of Abraham. His sons sold their brother Joseph into slavery out of envy of him, and told Jacob that he had been killed (Gen 37). Even though Joseph managed to become viceroy to the pharaoh in Egypt, he never, before his brothers came to Egypt in search of food during the seven-year famine, advised his father Jacob that he survived and had risen to power in Egypt.

Jethro. Midianite Priest and father of Zipporah, wife of Moses. According to tradition he was a monotheist and advisor to Pharaoh. Later, when the Israelites wandered in the desert, Jethro cautioned Moses to create a hierarchical judicial system, to lessen Moses' burden of adjudicating all disputes (Exod 14:13–26).

Joseph or **Joseph "the Righteous."** One of the twelve sons of the Patriarch Jacob, sold into slavery when his brothers became envious of him. A trusted advisor in the home of Potiphar, courtier of Pharaoh, falsely accused of sexually attacking Potiphar's wife and jailed. He later was released when he successfully interpreted the dreams of the then pharaoh, by predicting seven years of plenty to be followed by seven years of famine. Pharaoh named Joseph Zapheneth-Paneah, interpreted as "one who explains what is hidden," and appointed him Egypt's viceroy (Gen 41).

Joshua. Son of Nun. God's appointee to succeed Moses into the Promised Land (Num 27:18–23).

Kaballah. Mystical study of Judaism and its relationship to God.

Kashruth. Many commandments in the Torah are obligatory, even without explanation or logical basis—such as the laws of kashruth. The eating of a pig, for example, is forbidden because the pig does not have split hooves and does not chew its cud. No explanation is given as to why those physical characteristics logically bar the animal's edibility. The popular view that the pig is unclean, warranting the prohibition, however, is irrelevant to the traditionalist's view of the commandment. Under that view eating pig is forbidden simply because God said so. "Yet of those that chew the cud or have the hoof cleft you shall not eat these: the camel, the hare, and the rock badger, because they chew the cud but do not divide the hoof; they are unclean for you" (Deut 14:7).

Korah's Sons. The Book of Psalms or the Psalter contains a number of psalms (e.g., Nos. 44, 45, 46, 47, 48, 49), which, according to tradition, were authored by the "Sons of Korah." The Forty-Seventh Psalm is read in conjunction with the blowing of the ram's horn ("shofar") on Rosh Hashonah, the Jewish New Year—a call to repentance and contrition to earn God's forgiveness for the past year's sins (Num 29:1).

Noah. Lived ten generations after Adam and ten generations before Abraham at a time when the world was thoroughly corrupt. Being a righteous man who "walked with God," God directed him to build an ark to save civilization from a flood that would destroy all of the earth's inhabitants, man and animal, except the ark's occupants (Gen 6—8).

Og. King of Bashan. While wandering in the desert, the Israelites settled in the land of the Amorites and turned in the direction of Bashan. When Og attacked the Israelites, God told Moses not to fear him and Og was roundly defeated (Num 21:31–35).

Oral Tradition. According to the Ethics of the Fathers: "Moses received the Torah from Sinai and transmitted it to Joshua; Joshua to the Elders; the Elders to the Prophets; and the Prophets transmitted it to the Men of the Great Assembly" (*Ethics of the Fathers* 1:1). The Oral Tradition, which supplemented the written word in the Bible, the Prophets and the Holy Writings, according to this theory, was passed from generation to generation until Rabbi Judah the Prince began the editing process that committed the Oral Tradition to writing—first in the Mishna and then the Talmud which together comprise "the Oral Torah."

Potiphar. Joseph, who preceded the enslavement of the Hebrews, was jailed in Egypt after he rebuffed the sexual advances of the wife of Potiphar, courtier of Pharaoh. She falsely claimed that Joseph had sexually accosted her, resulting in his incarceration.

Red Heifer. According to the Torah, when someone touches the corpse of a human being he is contaminated for seven days. At the time when sacrifices were offered, he could purify himself with the collected ashes after the sacrifice of a completely red heifer that had been unblemished and had never worked (Num 19). The law of the Red Heifer is a quintessential law in the Torah that is "beyond human comprehension."

Rephidim. The Israelites complained against Moses at Rephidim asking "why is it that you have brought us up from Egypt to kill me and my children and my lifestock with thirst?" God told Moses to strike the rock and water would come forth, and it did (Exod 17:1–7).

Rest. The Sabbath is a day of consummate "rest," to commemorate that God rested on the seventh day in the week of Creation (Gen 2:1–6; Exod 20:9–11) ("the Fourth Commandment").

Sacred Ground. When Moses encountered the Burning Bush, God called to him from the Bush and said: "Do not come closer to here, remove your shoes from your feet, for the place upon which you stand is sacred ground" (Exod 3:4).

Sihon. King of the Amorites. While wandering for forty years in the desert, Israel's emissaries asked permission to pass through his borders. Sihon refused and waged war against Israel. Sihon and his people were smitten (Deut 2 and 3).

The Temple. The First Temple was built by King Solomon after the Israelites entered the Promised Land. It replaced the Tabernacle which was the movable house of worship and animal sacrifice, while the Israelites wandered in the desert. Solomon's Temple was destroyed by the Babylonians in 586 B.C.E. A Second Temple was later built on the same site, but destroyed by the Romans in 70 C.E. According to tradition, the Temples stood on Mount Moriah at the precise location where Abraham was willing to carry out God's direction to sacrifice his son. Since the destruction of the Second Temple by the Romans in 70 C.E., there has been no Temple and, consequently, no animal sacrifices. At the precise site now stands the Dome of the Rock, a primary Holy Site for Islam.

Terah. The father of Abraham, founder of monotheism (Gen 11:31). According to tradition, Terah was an idol worshipper and Abraham destroyed Terah's idols to prove that they were useless.

Wilderness of Sin. Here the Congregation complained that they suffered from famine. Hearing this, God rained down food from heaven in the form of manna (Exod 16:1–36).

Woman of Valor or **Women of Accomplishment.** A paean to valorous or accomplished women is contained in Proverbs 3.